THE SEVERAL LIVES OF PAUL FEJOS

Paul Fejos in 1959

THE
SEVERAL LIVES OF
PAUL FEJOS

A Hungarian-American

Odyssey

BY JOHN W. DODDS

THE WENNER-GREN FOUNDATION
1973

CONTENTS

INTRODUCTION

THIS IS THE STORY of a man who had more facets of intelligence, understanding, and accomplishment than are usually given to modern man, and who succeeded in bringing them all to a focus in a career for which the dubious word "unique" is entirely fitting.

It is also the record of a life which reached maturity, in the early century, in an age and environment which has so completely disappeared that it seems more "historical" than history. Some of the story lies in its Hungarian roots, some of it in a personality richly imaginative and creative (perhaps also Hungarian!), and some of it in a kind of acculturation to twentieth century America which was intensely real and functional and at the same time curiously detached and objective. Paul Fejos attained eminence in many fields, through a whole chain of improbable sequences, from the direction of motion pictures to the presidency, at last, of a foundation for anthropological research. He was not one man, but many. And everything he did he did well.

He was romantic and realistic, a man of sentiment and wittily sardonic, scientific and superstitious, modest but aware of his own abilities, rich in human kindness and warmth of friendship and yet sometimes prejudiced for what seemed accidental reasons. If you were his friend there was nothing, literally nothing, he would not try to do for you. If for some reason he mistrusted you he could be ineffably polite but cool. At the bottom of this was an intuition which saw through shams; but if they were decent shams he could tolerate them equably.

Like all human beings Paul Fejos was a walking paradox—seemingly a little more paradoxical than you or me, but this was a part of his complexity, which was in turn the matrix of his genius.

No pious "official" biography could explore properly the life of a man as talented, and as many-sided, as Paul Fejos. The main hope of this book will be to trace the several lives of a career for which it would be difficult to find parallels in the nature of its accomplishment (so much of it really *was* pioneering). But it is also the story of a fine human being who suffered, sometimes from himself, yet who was driven even by the accidents of his occasionally temperamental decisions into what, as one looks back on it, became a completely coherent pattern.

The Wenner-Gen Foundation absorbed Paul Fejos's time and attention during the last twenty-odd years of his life. This does not pretend to be a history of the Foundation itself, except as it became a part of Paul and he of it. Perhaps, for the record, foundation histories should be written. They would come alive, however, only as they might tell of *people*.

There are two main sources for this memoir. First, Paul Fejos in 1962 made some eight hours of taped interviews for the Oral History Collection at Columbia University. I am very grateful for those, and where it has been useful to do so I have let him tell the story in his own words. What he said was usually much more vivid than any paraphrase of it could be. He is in a true sense a collaborator in writing this history. It must be remembered, to be sure, that even in the shaping of his own life in words Paul was in a sense "staging" the account of his career. In more ways than one his life *was* a scenario, a reality to which his directorial instinct responded. He had a deep sense of what is fundamentally true, and he never violated that. In details, however, he has needed to be corrected at some points.

Paul talked in his interviews chiefly of his professional careers. He gave some of his opinions about the state of the world and particularly about anthropology, but little of what he said was highly personal. For that area of his life I am much indebted to Lita Osmundsen who, as his wife from 1958 to 1963, and as his collaborator in the work of the Wenner-Gren Foundation, knew him better than anyone else. Paul was a magnificent storyteller, and she remembered the stories! Without her this record would have been sadly incomplete.

Lothar Wolff, who knew him well in the thirties when he was making motion pictures in Europe (serving as his editor on a number of films), has been helpful in filling in details. Paul

Hanna contributed some interesting material about the Peruvian expedition. And it was good to have many of my impressions corroborated by such long-standing friends of Paul's as Iago Galdston and Anthony Sokol.

Still another source is my own knowledge of the man. As the writer of this sketch, therefore, I must enter the conventional claim of responsibility for my interpretations. I have tried to be as objective and to get at as much of the truth as I could about a very intricate personality. Yet at best the writing of a life is like looking at a fore-edge painting on a book: the viewer bends the volume a little to get what he hopes is the full perspective. If what I have written has in it a steady thread of affection and admiration, it is because no one who knew Paul well for twenty-two years could write otherwise.

Finally, I want to express my warm gratitude to Will T. Jones, both for reviewing the manuscript with his usual acuteness and helpfulness and for seeing it to press.

JOHN W. DODDS
Stanford, California
August 1, 1973

THE SEVERAL LIVES OF PAUL FEJOS

Chapter One

THE HUNGARIAN SURVIVES

———————————————◆•◆———————————————

D URING THE HOT SUMMER MONTHS of 1942 a man sat alone in a little office in Rockefeller Center trying to give away money which no one seemed to want. The sign on the door outside the secretary's small cubicle read "The Viking Fund." And Paul Fejos, the new director of this new philanthropic foundation, was working to establish contact with a number of wary American anthropologists. The Fund had been created for those anthropologists, but at the moment they didn't seem to believe in Santa Claus.

There were at the time some 750 anthropologists in the United States who were members of their national association.* They were not accustomed to special foundation attention. Nor was the Hungarian Fejos a conventional member of the anthropological guild. More damaging was the fact that the Viking Fund had recently been endowed to the extent of some two-and-a-half million dollars by the legendarily wealthy Swedish industrialist and entrepreneur Axel Wenner-Gren, a dimly sinister figure who was currently on the U.S. State Department blacklist for suspected collaboration with Göring and Hitler. The United States had been at war since the previous December, and anthropologists, as well as U.S. officialdom, were suspicious of the source of the foundation's capital and were puzzled about its possible purposes.

*There are more than 8,000 today. In the decade before the establishing of the Viking Fund, 165 Ph.D.'s were awarded in anthropology in the U.S.A. Between 1961 and 1970, 1257 Ph.D.'s were granted.

3

So Paul Fejos had few initial visitors; he was hoping wistfully
for applicants who would accept apparently dubious money.
It was his job first to assure American anthropology that the
Viking Fund was a legitimate enterprise, with its own impec-
cable American board of directors, free from any outside manipulation, and then to convince scholars that money was really
available for authentic anthropological research. This was a new
role for a man who had come back to the United States on Pearl
Harbor Day, and who in his 45 years had lived several careers,
each of them more exciting than his present anomalous one. He
had been a doctor of medicine, a research biological technician
under Dr. Simon Flexner, a motion-picture director, and a self-
taught ethnologist and archeologist. His motion pictures had
given him a distinguished reputation in both Europe and Hollywood. In his explorations he had photographed and collected new
ethnological information about little-known primitive tribes in
many parts of the world—Madagascar, the East Indies, East
Asia, the Amazon basin. He had uncovered buried Inca cities
above the Andean clouds. He was restless, creative, and imaginative—and the establishment of the Viking Fund had really been
the fulfillment of his own dream. But just now he sat behind the
clean desk in his small rented office and waited, a little lone-
somely, for someone to call his secretary for an appointment.

Paul Fejos was born in Budapest on January 24, 1897, the son
of Aurora Novélly and Desiré Fejos. He grew up in an Austro-
Hungarian Empire which was so very much pre-World-War I
that today it seems almost legendary. His family was Hungarian
gentry—the landed aristocracy—and although noble ("nemes")
it was without formal title. There was a deep family pride, however: it was the antiquity of a line, not its more recent titular
accessions, that counted. Thus the *Graf* Esterhazy line was more
honored than the *Prince* Esterhazy, for it was much older. The
Fejos ancestry could be traced back to the fifteenth century.
Desiré Fejos had also been commissioned as Captain in the Hussars; he was not expected to serve in the army, but he had the
position which went with the rank. Paul's mother too came from
an old and distinguished family—more recently it had included

4

Francis Déak, the great nineteenth century Hungarian states-
man. She had served as court lady ("Palast Dame") for the
Empress Elisabeth, the beautiful wife of Franz Joseph.

Paul's earliest summers were spent at the family estate at
Szekszard, the winters in Budapest. He never knew his father,
who died when the boy was two. His mother and her two children (he had one sister) then went to live with her grandfather's
brother and his wife; Paul called him "Grandfather." He adored
this man, just as he worshipped his mother, and just as he lived
within the memory of what he thought his father had been.
These early years were warm and secure, in a period and a
country which seemed to give peace and order, and to lend the
assurance that next year things would be just the same as they
were now.

There were more difficult times ahead. When his "grandfather" died the management of the family came under the
control of Paul's uncle (his father's younger brother), whom
he grew to fear and despise. The uncle was a stern Victorian-
Hungarian who had disliked Paul's father, whom he considered
"wild." He sent Paul to a Jesuit school, saying that he needed
"discipline." (Paul, incidentally, always liked and respected the
Jesuits for their intellectual liberalism.)

Paul's nightmares were always full of his uncle. The man
was some sort of judge, and at one time Minister of Justice, pom-
pous and self-righteous. Sometimes he would appear at lunch
dressed in a manner which indicated that he was to sentence
someone to death that afternoon—a role which, Paul thought,
he obviously enjoyed. One day standing on the balcony after
lunch Paul and his young cousin saw a man who had been on
trial being driven past the house. "He is going to be hung," said
the cousin. "Yes," said the uncle, who had appeared behind the
boys, pointing at Paul, "and that will be your fate some day,
young man." As long as he lived Paul never saw a movie which
involved a hanging without getting physically ill, so deep-seated
was his resultant trauma.

The family crisis reached a peak when, in his last year in the
Gymnasium, Paul declared that he had fallen in love with the
theater, and wanted to work in it. This was unthinkable for a

5

Fejos; the family status would have suffered terribly. Law, yes; the army, yes; medicine, yes, for that was a gentleman's profession, if one didn't make money by it—but the theater, never! The family was prepared (literally) to bring in a physician to test the boy's sanity. Finally, in council they said in effect: "All right. If you want this so much, first get a diploma. And if you have one and you still are crazy, then you can go ahead and do what you want."

So the young Fejos went to medical school, though a war intervened before he got his degree.

Already Paul was revealing the traits which were to be his throughout life: a stubborn determination to be his own man—an insistence on personal identity not unlike the intense demand of all Hungarians for the recognition of the special authenticity of their national culture. Paul was in a sense *outside* his culture —a maverick, or at least in rebellion against the structured Victorian overlay which possessed his immediate environment. In many respects, however, he can be understood only in the context of his origins, no matter how much sea-change he underwent later. Wherever he went in future years he always tried to build a cultural cocoon around him (we shall see some of them), to create little links with the past. One basic quality was an intense pride (not vanity) which was combined with a deep sense of honor and responsibility—to others, to himself, and thus to the code by which he lived. His sense of values might sometimes seem to others eccentric, but at bottom it had its own rationale and its own integrity. It included stamina and bravery and generosity and *noblesse oblige*, and the determination to face up to the results of even your aberrant behavior.

Above all, it involved The Gesture, and also, importantly, the necessity of paying the price for it. No one must be allowed to top you in generosity, bravery, your sense of manhood. But if you promised the world, you had to deliver the world, preferably in style. For the gesture was really a kind of life-style—emotional, dramatic, spontaneous with a sort of controlled spontaneity.

One small example at the moment. In Paul's movie days, the beautiful Annabella was once one of his leading women—very

6

probably he had an affair with her. She had played the leading part in *Marie* (1932), the one of Paul's Hungarian films which he liked best. When Annabella was leaving Hungary, Paul flew over her train (he was also an aviator) and strewed bushels of roses in front of the engine. People talked about it for a long time.

In a sense Paul inherited the gesture and the code that went with it from his father. The legend ran that at one time at the Fejos country estate, as guests were leaving after a party, the flares which were to light them to their carriages did not materialize. So the father ordered a servant to set fire to the ripe wheat in the near fields—it was harvest time—and the guests were sent brilliantly on their way.

Earlier, when Paul's father was courting his mother, she once said impatiently that he wouldn't give his little finger for her. Whereupon he marched to the kitchen, seized a meat cleaver, and cut off his little finger in proof of his devotion. Whether or not he presented it to her is not in the record. Pixilated, but in the grand manner.

Paul always felt a kinship with Rostand's Cyrano de Bergerac; he never could understand how such a man, who should have been Hungarian, was a mere Gascon. Many of the Cyranic traits were Paul's (except the hopeless love for one woman): the concern for his good name, the bravery—and the showmanship which made the bravery clear to all—the romantic idealism, the loyalty, the wit and the bravado, the despair, the indomitable, poetic clinging to the image one creates. He, like Cyrano, hated to contemplate dying in a chair. Like Cyrano he would have liked, when he entered before God, to have his salute "sweep all the stars away from the blue threshold." Cyrano was The Gesture epitomized. Paul never created a *ballade*, as Cyrano did, while dueling, but he did sometimes in Hungary carve his initials on his opponent's chest—his own kind of poetic sentiment. He was Cyrano's spiritual brother—however subdued much of it might have seemed to those who knew him in his later years.

Paul enrolled at the Royal Hungarian Medical University in Budapest, but by 1917 he was in the cavalry in World War I, with the 7th Hussars.

7

He had ridden since he was a small boy, and it seemed only natural, when he first reported to his colonel and the colonel asked "Do you ride?" to say, "Yes, sir." "Oh, you do?" said the colonel, turning to his aide and saying, "I've been riding for 35 years, and if anyone were to ask me if I knew anything about riding, I would not have the temerity to say I did. Assign him Wilma for his horse."

So Paul got Wilma, a liberated female with a mind of her own. Each day on the parade ground it was the ritual for each member of a unit to ride up to the colonel very fast, report, and ride back to his unit. Paul, in his turn, rode Wilma up to the colonel—and kept going right past! He tried again and the same thing happened. Wilma would stop only when she decided to. Paul was the laughing stock of the group for some time.

Another episode involved the Sunday morning parade when the company was riding to church in a little town where they were in barracks. It was the custom, as they rode thus in formation, for the men to give a certain formal, sabre-drawing salute to people of importance they might pass, such as the wives of the high officers. Occasionally, if an officer liked a young lady, the company would perform the same salute for her, and the commander would wink at the infraction of the hierarchal rule.

One rainy Sunday as they rode past the local candy store, a young girl whom Paul liked was standing there at her door. He decided that his group might as well give her the big salute. But the wet street was paved with rough cobblestones, with a very high crown, and just as they got to the point of drawing sabres a little dog came yapping out under the heels of Paul's horse. The horse shied and then slid sideways down into the gutter, landing on top of Paul, in the mud, while the platoon had to keep riding on past.

He never saw the girl again.

Even in World War I the cavalry was obsolescent for effective military operation. Paul's company was used only for reconnaissance. Small patrols would go out; one man would ride into a town and then turn swiftly and gallop away. If no one in the town got nervous and shot, it could be guessed that the town was safe.

8

Before long he had made the transition from horse cavalry to air cavalry, and soon was flying a plane down the Italian mountain corridors, again for reconnaissance purposes. The planes were not armed, though sometimes the pilot would toss a cluster of hand-grenades out of the cockpit at some likely target. It was important, too, not to get caught in a rain, lest the shellac on the cloth wings should dissolve and leave the pilot flapping helplessly in the air. It was all pretty primitive by any modern standards—and hazardous.

Paul was discharged in 1919, after the Communists under Bela Kun had seized power in Hungary. He returned to medical school and received his degree in 1921; the university had allowed certain credits for time spent in the army. By then most of the family property had been lost. When the war began in 1914 Paul's mother, who had never remarried, decided to sell the estate and buy the Hungarian equivalent of American "Liberty Bonds." Those of course became totally worthless at the end of the war when the revolution broke out. The mother's greatest regret was that Paul would now have to work for a living.

So he was not only relieved from any pressure to become a country gentleman; he actually had to scramble for a job. He had no desire to practice medicine,* and his way was now clear to continue with the theater and motion pictures. Indeed even while he was finishing medical school he directed several films for the newly-organized Mobil Studios. In 1919 he directed *Pan*, a mythological story with Claire Bauroff. The same year he did *Lord Arthur Seville's Crime (Lidércnyomas)*. In 1920 *The Black Captain (Fekete Kapitany,)* a melodrama about crooked police in New York City, which Paul had never seen; and a film called *Reincarnation (Ujraélok)*. And in 1921 *Arsène Lupin's Last Adventure (Arsène Lupin Utolso Kalandja)*; *The Stars of Eger (Egri Csillagok)*, which was a dramatization of Geza Gardonyi's novel about the Turkish domination of Hungary; and a film version of Pushkin's *Pique Dame*.

During this period, presumably, he was completing his medi-

*In fact he never did practice medicine, except on field trips when he would care for the illnesses and injuries of natives and members of the expedition. He always kept up on the subject, however—took in and read the professional magazines and knew what was happening in modern medicine.

cal studies. One wonders how he had time for all this, but the pictures were all short and in all probability not too distinguished. "We made those pictures in a week and had a lot of fun," he recalled later. He was on an apprentice's way toward the career he had set for himself.

He used to tell some amusing anecdotes about those early films. In one of them the big scene was a headon crash between two locomotives. All the elaborate preparations were made, and the accident was a spectacular success—a burst of steam, fire, and flying metal. Later, on the train going back to the city, Paul, much pleased with the sequence, noticed that his cameraman was sitting glumly and silently in the corner. At last the man admitted that he had forgotten to take the lens cap off the camera!

Even at this time Paul was fascinated by America, and his one picture about the United States, *The Black Captain*, must have given Hungarians an even stranger impression of that distant country than they already had. The plot required some U.S. policemen to rap the curbstone with their nightsticks. Paul had never seen a nightstick—it never occurred to him they were made of *wood*—and so he stuffed some leather sticks with sawdust. When the policemen pounded the curbs sawdust flew in all directions. The result was a Mack Sennett effect in a film meant to be serious.

Between 1921 and 1923 Paul staged a number of plays and operas in Budapest and plays in Paris, one of them at the *Grand Guignol* theatre. He was in the Max Reinhardt *genre*, and for a time worked with Reinhardt in a technical capacity; he developed a new means of creating a fire on stage. In 1922 he directed a Passion Play in a small Hungarian village with a cast of hundreds of persons, none of whom could read. The lines had to be spoken to them until they memorized them. He became director for a time of an advanced French theater, where he had every freedom in the staging of plays. He produced, among others, Walter Hasenclever's expressionistic *L'Homme*, in something like sixty-four scenes.

In October 1921, Paul had married Mara Jankowsky in Budapest. She was an actress and a very lovely girl—of "the early Joan Bennett type," if one wants to draw a cinematic parallel.

Their few years together were tempestuous ones. Paul was quick to anger, like many Hungarians, but he was also inordinately jealous, suspicious of almost any man his wife glanced at. (This was true all his life.) He fought something like five duels on behalf of what seemed to him his good name and marital honor. After two years the attractive Mara decided that she couldn't stand this any longer. They separated in 1923 and were divorced in August 1924, after Paul had gone to New York.

His reasons for leaving for the United States were complex. Hungary was greatly disturbed politically and economically during the early twenties, and Paul had always been immensely curious about America. One suspects, however, that the separation from his wife was an inciting cause. One notices throughout his career, indeed, how frequently a change in that career was tied in with the collapse of a love affair. There were always other, more or less logical, reasons for the shifts, but somehow they often coincided with matters of the heart.

On October 15, 1923, Paul arrived at New York on the *Leviathan*. There was a background of confused family conception about the United States: it was very far away and there were Indians there, and the citizens were great bluffers and hoaxers —not too honest. When he left, his mother begged him not to go too far from New York lest the Indians kill him.

He landed with a few hundred dollars and a letter of introduction to a Hungarian banker in New York, given him by a Budapest banker. He had no idea how anyone made money in the United States. Presumably you got a job, but how, and what did you do? The letter to the banker proved nonproductive; the man kept him waiting an hour in his anteroom. Paul believed that he had thus been contemptuously insulted (he explained this later as "a cultural thing") and left without even seeing the banker. Once his anger had cooled he couldn't go back and apologize: that was part of the code.

What to do? He returned to the Waldorf-Astoria, where he had gone upon landing, for a man of importance, he understood, stayed only at the Waldorf. He counted his money; by now he had $5.10 left. He took off his cufflinks, took his wallet and cigaret case, and went out to find a pawnshop. On of his funnier

11

stories was about how a German told him to look on Sixth Avenue for a shop with three balls in front of it.

He knew little English; his vocabulary at the time was chiefly "Yes," "Thank you," and "All right." He was completely and utterly a foreigner and alone. Even his name was a hazard in this new culture. Later, when he was getting his first citizenship papers, as he told it:

"The clerk insisted 'Full name.' So I said, 'Paul Fejos,' and he said, 'No middle name?' I said, 'Yes.' 'Well, let's have the middle name.' I said, 'There are too many.' 'Well, let's have them.' And it happens that I have seven middle names and they end up in the word Marie, because this is given to many children in Hungary, which is a highly Catholic country. And unfortunately the man who sat there taking all this down thought that I was kidding and got very mad and started to scream at me: 'This is an official place, and you're not supposed to make jokes!' And I said, 'But I'm not joking. My last middle name is really Marie.' He called a policeman from the corridor and it took me quite a long time to explain and show by my birth certificate that it was really my name."

The story of the early, baffling days in New York, the subsequent period of success, and finally the transition to Hollywood, can best be told in Paul's own words. He was always apologetic about what he called his "baseball English." As a matter of fact few people spoke more vividly, or occasionally eloquently, than he.

"Then came a rather bitter period of about three months, in 1923. I wanted to work but I hadn't the slightest idea where or how to find work. To compensate for this, I believe, every morning I got up at 6:30 for no reason—I am normally a late riser—but I needed to show myself that I was trying. I lived on 72nd Street West, and I started out every morning from there and walked clear down to the Battery and then walked back from the Battery again, which is a long, long distance. During the time of all these walks, I had the wildest daydreams. I thought that somebody would suddenly look at me on the street, stop me, and tell me this is the man they wanted since I don't know when.

None of these wild dreams, of course, came to fruition, except one single time.

"I walked one day somewhere in midtown and heard music, band music, and went toward the music. And when I arrived the street was jammed with people; mounted police were there, music played, and the crowd sort of pushed me forward, until finally I arrived at the middle of this crowd where there was an empty circle. And just as I stepped out there, a gentleman in a high hat and a cutaway up on a brownstone stoop lifted his hat, looked at me, and started to talk in English that I did not understand.

"So there was a fulfillment of this crazy dream: Here I was being fêted finally after arriving in New York. Later on, I found out that this was the house where Theodore Roosevelt was born, and on that day they had some sort of a jubilee, and the man was not waiting for me, of course, but for the arriving deputation behind me.

"I finally learned from an unknown man, to whom I owe a great deal, how to get a job. I walked my regular walk from the Battery back to 72nd Street and got to Union Square, and as I was tired I decided to sit down on a bench for a minute. After a few seconds of sitting on the bench, a man rather poorly dressed, without a tie, came over and sat down next to me on the bench. After about two minutes he said something in English, which, of course, I did not understand. But I understood one word: 'cigarette.'

"So I thought the man wanted a cigarette and pulled out cigarettes and handed them to him. He took one and started to talk. I had great difficulty understanding him, so I just told him, 'I don't speak English. I don't understand.' He turned to me and asked me if I am Italian and I said, 'No.' Am I German? I said, 'No, but I do speak German.' 'Oh, I speak German, too.' Then I found out that he had been in the American Occupation Army in Germany, and had picked up some words there.

"Then he said something about the beautiful day that we were having and such things, and I was puzzled by one thing: How was it that this man at 11 o'clock, in the forenoon, had time to sit here? I had learned that in America everybody works. How

13

come that this man could sit here? And then I asked him. He said, 'Well, I had a job this forenoon, and I will get one tomorrow. I still have enough money,' and he reached in his pocket and pulled out a bunch of small change, I think about $1.20, or something like that. He said, 'This will hold until tomorrow. Tomorrow I will get another job.'

"Here was the miraculous thing, that somebody knew how to get a job. So I asked him. Then he told me, 'It's very simple. You go at midnight out to the street and buy the *New York World* and then look up the section in the small ads called 'Men Wanted,' and then take any job that you like.' I said, 'But do they give it to you?' and he said, 'Sure.' 'But I don't know anything, I don't know how to work.' I didn't want to tell him I was a doctor. He said, 'That doesn't matter. If they kick you out they pay you for the time that you spend there,' which was for me a terrific innovation; I never heard of a thing like that. And then he told me, 'Yesterday, I was a welder.' He got the job in the morning at 8 o'clock. 'They fired me at 10:30, but I got the money for the time that I spent there.' This seemed really a magic land, where you get a job, you get fired, and still they pay you.

"That evening I went out at midnight on Columbus Circle and bought the *New York World* and looked up the 'Men Wanted' column, carefully avoiding any advertisement which started out with 'Strong man wanted,' because my friend from Union Square had warned me not to go for a job like that because it meant very heavy work. I found one job which I decided to look for, because the job was in a theater, and that was just up my alley. It simply said, 'Young man wanted for theatrical work. No experience necessary. Apply at 7 in the evening, stage entrance, Winter Garden.'

"That evening I went over to the Winter Garden, and again, through the advice of my friend from the park, I went early, because he told me, 'Go very early. The first man gets the job.' And then I found a little iron door—the iron door is still there, though the Winter Garden looks different now—and after about five or ten minutes waiting, the door opened and a hand came out—not a man, but just an arm and a hand, reached over and grabbed me by the shoulder and yanked me in. At the same time, the man behind the hand yelled something in English for the rest of them. Now, I know now what he yelled was, 'You can all go away; the job is filled.' And then he motioned me to come after him, and after we went through a long, tunnel-like corridor which led onto the stage of the Winter Garden, there stood three other men. One of them, obviously the foreman, came over, looked at me, and said something in English—again I could not understand one word—so very meekly I just said, 'No speak English, please.'

"Immediately this man burst out in a terrific scolding and bawled the daylight out of the poor man who pulled me in and pointed toward the tunnel, obviously telling the guy to go out and try to get somebody else. The man went and came back with the obvious; there was no one out there.

"So I got the job, which made me the man who woke up the sun over Manhattan. The Winter Garden then had one glass wall which faced the audience, who also ate and drank there, and it was a glass sheet replica of the New York skyline. From the sea the sun was supposed to come out, in certain cycles, go high above New York, stop at noon for a while; and then a terrific storm started with rain and lightning and darkness, and then on the other side, the sun went down. The mechanism which was transporting this large reflector which was the sun was out of kilter. They needed me while this was being repaired. I got a pair of asbestos gloves and there were ladders lashed together with rope. I climbed up to the top of this and then climbed down on the other side, holding with the asbestos gloves this reflector which was hot and smelled to high heaven. To push it up was not difficult but to come down with it was extremely inconvenient because one held it almost in one's lap and got all the heat.

"Anyhow for the enormous sum of $12 weekly and also food, (which was food that came back from the plates), I had the job.

"They explained to me that I should push this sun up and let it down, and it must be very even. This was explained in English with a lot of gestures, and I understood it. And anyhow, at that time, when anybody said anything to me, I always said, 'Yes,' immediately, and 'Please.'

"This job lasted exactly two weeks. Two weeks later the job was finished and then I went again to the *New York World* and found another ad: 'Distinguished young man wanted. Must have cutaway,' and there was an address under it. It was an advertisement of the Campbell Funeral Home on Broadway and 71st. They needed, so to speak, professional mourners. So I got this job. For this I needed to speak English. It was only one sentence but it was very difficult to learn because it contained a 'w.' I needed to say, 'Watch your step, please.' From one chapel to another, it was a step downward. I stood there seven hours a day, seeing endless funerals, and saying to everybody coming in, 'Watch your step, please.' It was exceedingly difficult to learn the 'w' in 'Watch your step, please,' and say it without a 'v.'

"This lasted again two weeks, because I was substituting for one of the people who was employed there steadily and who was on vacation. However, this paid $16 a week. When that was over, a day later I heard that they were taking workers at the Winter Piano Factory in the Bronx. I walked over there, and as one was not supposed to wear a necktie, I took my necktie off before I went in, and got there a job as a day-laborer for, if I am right, $18 a week.

"My first month there was spent in carrying player pianos on my back, which was very hard work, but today I'm grateful for it. Then a month later I advanced to the assembly section of pianos. These were player pianos and they worked with air power from a bellows that one pushed with one's foot, and I threaded on rubber tubings inside these pianos. This lasted until the spring of 1924.

"I usually worked every day from 7 until 5, but on Saturdays it was 7 until 3 in the afternoon, and my leisure time was spent on 14th Street, which then was nearer the center of Manhattan and had ten-cent stores. And, of course, the ten-cent stores were a wonder for me because you would see a million different kinds of merchandise and toward the end of the store were radios. Radio was a new invention; loudspeakers were blaring out music, plus at the end of the store there was always a piano with a girl who played current tunes. If you wanted to buy music, the girl played it first.

"I spent a lot of time in these ten-cent stores, having this terrific entertainment. And then slowly I discovered that New York had other entertainments which are free. I found out that there is a Metropolitan Museum and a lot of other things.

"One day, coming home from 14th Street, somewhere in midtown I think it was, 48th Street or something like that, I passed a house which had a sign over it which said, 'The Chemists' Club.' I decided to look into the vestibule and went in, and there was a big blackboard on which was an announcement that Dr. So and So this afternoon is giving a paper on different amino compounds, or something similar. Well, I didn't know much organic chemistry but I knew some and I decided that I would go in and listen to this because it was written, 'Admission free,' which I knew meant that I didn't need to pay, and I knew that this program might help me, not with chemistry but with my English, 'because certainly this man who lectures here must be somebody who speaks good English.'

"So I went in and listened to a highly boring lecture, which I did not understand. After the lecture I filed out again into the vestibule and then I saw a small sign on a door which said, 'Employment Bureau of the Chemists' Club.' I knocked on the door, opened it, and went in, and found a very young lady behind the desk, chewing gum viciously, and she said something like, 'What's yours?' or 'What can I do for you?' And I told her that I would like to get a job. Am I a chemist? I said, 'No, I am not. I am a medical doctor, and I am not thinking of getting employment in a chemical firm, but I thought that maybe a clinical laboratory could use me.' She pulled out a sheet of paper and handed it over and said, 'Fill it out.' The form had places for my name, where was I born, what degrees, and all that. I filled out everything carefully mentioning again that I was not a chemist but that I could do pathological stains, urine analysis, blood chemistry and so on. Well, the lady took this back from me and said, 'Five dollars, please.' I had altogether eight dollars and some cents, but to pay out five dollars meant that I wouldn't have

17

subway money to go to work. So I said to the woman, 'I'm sorry. I did not know that this would cost money. I can pay now three dollars and later I'll bring in the other two.'

"She broke out into terribly fast abuse, in English which I couldn't get, but I understood that she was very angry with me. It seems that these application charts were numbered and she had to account for each chart. She raised her voice quite high, and suddenly a door opened on the side, and a small man entered, who turned to the girl and said, 'What seems to be the trouble?' The girl broke out again with terrific abuse: 'This man comes here, takes one of the blanks, fills it out, and now doesn't want to pay, and I need to account for it!'

"I broke in and said, 'I'm sorry, but the lady is not telling the exact truth. It is not that I don't want to pay; I shall pay, but the full payment I can make only one week from now, because I don't have enough money.'

"This man turned to me and said, 'May I have that application,' and he looked at it and then looked up at me and said, 'Are you a medical doctor?' and I said, 'Yes.' 'Do you have your diploma?' I said, 'Yes, but I don't have it with me; it's at home.' 'Could you bring it in this afternoon?' I said, 'Certainly.' But I told him, 'It's in Latin; I don't know if it will do any good.' 'Oh, just bring it in.' So I brought it in. He looked it through; then he said to me, 'What are you doing now?' I said, 'I'm working in a piano factory.' 'What are you doing?' 'Day-labor.'

"He said, 'Well, I tell you what. Just leave this with me and you will hear from me.' I left the place and when I went out I thought he simply meant to get rid of me. To my great amazement, two days later, on Tuesday morning, the landlady of the rooming house where I lived screamed at the top of her lungs that I had a telegram. I went downstairs and there was a telegram which said, 'Please appear on Wednesday forenoon, between the hours of 10 to 12, at the office of Dr. Flexner,' and under it was signed, 'Rockefeller Institute.'

"Well, my first reaction was to tear the telegram up, because what could I do at Rockefeller Institute? This is ridiculous! But then I though better of it and Wednesday when I went to the factory I had a clean shirt on and after about 15 minutes I went to the foreman and said, 'I have an awful toothache, please let me go for an hour until I can get it attended to.' He let me out and I went over to the corner of Avenue A and 66th Street—which was then the address of the Rockefeller Institute—and I walked in and there was a page boy. I handed the telegram over and to my greatest amazement, the page boy said, 'Doctor,' and 'Yes, sir,' and 'No, sir,' and showed me to the place where I was to sit down.

"Then I was ushered into the office of the business manager, who again treated me as a human being, not as 'Hey, you,' and said, 'Dr. Flexner wishes to see you. However, he is tied up now. Would you mind sitting down.' By this time my Hungarian anger at being made to wait had subsided, so I sat down and waited for about 20 minutes. Then I was ushered through a small tunnel at the end of which was an old building of the Rockefeller Institute. I was carried up in an elevator to the fourth floor, and taken into a room where there was a secretary who said, 'Please sit down in the library. Dr. Flexner will see you at once.' The whole thing seemed like a dream.

"After about five minutes an elderly gentleman came in, with white hair and very skinny. This was Dr. Simon Flexner. I knew that he was the discoverer of the *Bacillus flexneri*, and had done a lot of work on dysentery and other diseases. He asked me to sit down, offered me a smoke and said, 'Well, you are the M.D. who is doing piano work.' I said, 'Yes.' He said, 'What are you doing? Tuning the pianos?' I said, 'No. Assembling them.' 'How did you get to do that?' I said, 'That was the only work I could get.' He asked, 'What do you earn?' So I told him—at that time it was relatively high—'I earn $20 a week.' Then he said to me, 'Do you like this work?' I said, 'Not particularly.' 'Why don't you work in a hospital or somewhere?' I said, 'Because I don't speak enough English. I couldn't speak to patients; I wanted a laboratory job but couldn't get it.'

"He said, 'So you live on $20 a week.' I said, 'Yes,'—and since I did not want to lie—told him I had a side income. After about four or five months I found out that in Central Park people rode horseback and that these horses came from stables all around Central Park. I went to one of the stables on Seventh Avenue and

walked in and asked them if I could exercise their horses;
I'd do it for nothing. If on Saturday afternoons I could exercise
horses I would be very grateful. The man who was there said,
'Well, why?' I said, 'Because I have ridden all my life and I miss
it.' 'Since when have you ridden?' I said, 'Since I was four
years old.'

"So he motioned one of the people who brought forth a horse
which was already saddled, and he turned to me and said,
'Mount it.' I got into the saddle and then he said, 'Okay, you can
come down.' He said, 'All right. We can't tell you when, but if
you come Saturday afternoon, always at 2 o'clock, if there are
any horses to be exercised, you can take them out.' I told Flexner
that occasionally I got from this place $5, $3 a week, as tips from
people whom I took around the park, because they were sometimes short of instructors and so I would go out with somebody.

"When I told him this he said, 'What are you? Are you a
doctor? Are you a horseback rider? Are you a piano maker?' I
said, 'I'd do most anything just to be able to live.' 'Well,' he
said, 'I will call somebody in and we'll find out, maybe we can
help you.' He got on the phone, and then a few minutes later a
gentleman came in, to whom I was introduced—he was Professor Bronfenbrenner. Professor Bronfenbrenner was a bacteriologist from the Pasteur Institute who had come to Rockefeller to
do research. While we were waiting for Bronfenbrenner, Flexner
asked me just how well I rode horseback. I said, 'The same way
any Hussar would.' 'Well, what does that mean? Does it mean
more than just to be in control of the horse?' I said, 'Yes, it means
also vaulting, cutting telegraph wire and all that.' 'How do you
cut telegraph wire?' I said, 'You get up in the saddle, stand on
it, and then you just cut the wire.' 'You mean you can stand on
a horse?' I said, 'Yes, of course; I mean, that is almost elemen-
tary.'

"I impressed him greatly, and when Bronfenbrenner came in,
he said, 'Now meet him. This is the young man who is in a piano
factory, can ride a horse standing on it,' and I don't know what
else. I didn't feel very good. I felt that they were poking fun at
me, but they were not. Finally he turned to me and said, 'You
go with Dr. Bronfenbrenner and he'll question you about some

20

other things.' So I knew, 'Here it is coming and I will be kicked out in five minutes.'

"I went to the laboratory of Bronfenbrenner, sat down, and he asked me first about what I was able to do. I told him, 'I can stain bacteria, I can take care of cultures, I can do some blood chemistry, can do different physiological analyses.' He listened to all that and said, 'Well, what do you earn now?' I said, '$20 a week.' He said, 'Well, then I don't know if you want to come here, because if we take you here as a technician, your starting salary will be $20 a week, $80 a month.' I told him it wouldn't matter; I would do this rather than to be in a factory. So he said to me, 'All right. When can you start?' I said, 'Anytime.' He said, 'Tomorrow?' I said, 'Tomorrow.'

"The next morning, I did not go to the factory but went straight to the Rockefeller Institute and was no end pleased by the treatment everybody accorded me. I was set to work by Bronfenbrenner, and then the troubles began. I suddenly found out I knew nothing. He came into the lab with a small test tube containing some yellow liquid and said to me, 'This is *botulinus* toxin. I want you to titrate this in mice, intracranially, and give me the minimum MLD (Minimum Lethal Dose).' Number one, I did not know that a toxin called *botulinus* existed. Next, I did not know how one titrates a toxin. I did not know how you titrated intracranially, into the head. And I hadn't the slightest idea what MLD is. So I went back to my lab with this mysterious liquid, sat down and sat there for a full hour, looking at it. I didn't know what to do next.

"Finally, I decided the best thing to do was to go back and tell them I was just a faker; 'I don't know anything about this, kick me out.' I started out toward the door and the door opened and Bronfenbrenner walked in, turned to me, and said, 'Why aren't you working?' I told him. He said, 'Well, you should have asked questions.' I told him I didn't dare. 'Oh, ridiculous. Nobody knows everything.' And then he said, 'Come on with me,' and he took me to the Institute's library and said, 'If you ever want to look something up, any reference, this is the library.' He called the Librarian, Dr. Trask, introduced me, and from then on I spent many nights in the library.

21

"So I finally learned that MLD means minimum lethal dose, and that's the reason you titrate the toxin and you titrate it on animals. I think I was never so happy in my life as in the Rockefeller Institute. It was a job where I liked what I was doing. I was doing research. It was tremendously exciting. I had no worries, no responsibilities. It was gentlemanly and scholarly work. I really think it was the happiest period of my whole life."

At this time there was a small Hungarian colony of intellectuals and artists in New York which centered on a salon run by Charlotte Lederer, an elderly Hungarian lady who was the mother of Anna M. Rosenberg. Mrs. Rosenberg later had a distinguished career in the U.S. government, serving at one time, 1950-53, as Assistant Secretary of Defense. The expatriates who met at the Lederer home had a kind of identity; it was difficult to explain to outsiders a language and a way of life which few understood. Paul moved in and out of this society. It was probably there that he met Nicolas Muray, later to become a famous photographer and one of Paul's best friends. They often used to fence together. In general, however, he never sought out Hungarians because they were Hungarians. Many of them he didn't like. He reprehended what he called their bluffing (of which he was fully capable himself)—but bluffing without being prepared to have their bluffs called.

However much he enjoyed his work he must have been lonely and a little frightened during these years. He was no snob, but he felt that life somehow should have grace, a grace which had belonged to the ordered social structure he had known as a youth. He distilled what elements of this he could into his own little cultural island in a strange country. One of his old friends at the Rockefeller Institute, Dr. Philip Reichert, remembers a dinner that Paul served him in the little room he was then living in, a room without much furnishing except a bed and a night-table. He had put two orange crates together as a dining-table. He and his friend sat on the side of the bed, and on the crates Paul had placed a cloth and two silver dishes and a candle. He had cooked a marvelous dinner on a two-burner gas stove, and the little dinky room was somehow lighted up with *style* which had its own beautiful identity.

Paul goes on:
"This lasted until the end of 1925. Earlier in the year one of the page boys at the Institute came over to me and said, 'There is a gentleman downstairs in the vestibule waiting for you,' and handed me a visiting card. I looked at the card; the name meant nothing to me. I said, 'All right. Tell the gentleman I will be with him in a few minutes.' I was up in surgery assisting Dr. Carrel, so I couldn't get out, but as soon as the surgery was finished, I walked out to see this man. His name was Lee Simonson, and he was then the set designer of the Guild Theatre. I didn't know him and I walked over and I said, 'Are you looking for me?' He said, 'No.' 'Well,' I said, 'the boy just brought up this card.' He looked and said, 'Well, it must be some mistake. I am looking for a Paul Fejos who is a film director.' So I said, 'Yes, it must be that. What is it?' He said, 'We are putting on a production of Ferenc Molnár's called *The Glass Slipper* and we're having an awful lot of trouble with local color. We don't know what a Hungarian bath house looks like inside, we don't know how a Hungarian policeman is dressed. And these gypsies, how are gypsies dressed?'

"He showed me a letter. It was from Molnár saying that they should look me up; that I could give them all the information.* From that point on, I spent quite a lot of time away from the Institute and in the Guild, attending rehearsals, and to my greatest amazement I found out that people started to understand what I was saying. Up to that period I knew that nobody understood me. You see, one of the great difficulties with my English learning was that at the Rockefeller Institute, where I hoped to learn English, everybody was a foreigner. Hyodo Houchi was Japanese, Carrel was French, Landsteiner was Austrian. There a staff

---

The Glass Slipper was produced October 14, 1925. Paul knew Molnár reasonably well. He admired him greatly as a dramatist (they both had something of the same feeling for the realistic-fantastic), but he deplored Molnár's stinginess—not a typical Hungarian trait. Paul used to say that Molnár invented the phrase: "Separate checks, please."

23

meeting sounded like a babble; everybody spoke with a different accent. So I never realized that I had an accent, and it took me ten more years to learn that I don't speak the same way as other people.

"Anyhow this gave me in one way a terrific push, because seeing how I was accepted at the Guild by all the actors and everybody else and how they listened to everything I said, I thought that maybe it was time for me to try to break into theater or films in the United States. And once this idea lodged in my head, I couldn't get rid of it."

Chapter Two

ONE CAREER: A SUCCESS STORY

———————◆•◗——————

P AUL'S BREAK FROM New York toward Hollywood was of
course the result of his own deep-seated professional drives.
It so happened, however, that it coincided with a second
marriage, curious and baffling to one who didn't know Paul. In
the summer of 1925, while he was still at the Institute, he had
occasion to spend some time at Woods Hole, then as now an important biological research center. There he met Mimosa Pfaltz,
a German-American woman and a chemist. As Paul told the
story, they went on a boat ride and he leaned over and kissed her.
She asked, "When are we getting married?", and he didn't know
how to get out of it—the Code rose in his face: you always carried out your responsibilities, express or implied. They were
married in November; Paul lived with her for thirty days. They
were formally separated on May 28, 1929 and were divorced on
September 9th of the same year in Nevada. He paid alimony
to her until the month he died, thirty-four years later.

Paul again takes up the story:
"So in 1926, sometime I believe in late spring, I decided that
it was time to break into Hollywood, which was some 3,000 miles
away. I went to Dr. Flexner—may he forgive me—and I lied to
him. I gave him a long story that for family reasons I must go
to California, and therefore I wanted to resign, and would he
please let me go. He said yes, and I think he was really sorry
that I was leaving. He asked me if I had any connections in California. I said, 'None.' 'Oh, well,' he said, 'then we'll help you.
Come back to the office two weeks from now, and maybe I'll have
something for you, some news.' Two weeks later he called me

into the office and told me that I could have an appointment as an instructor in bacteriology at the University of California in Berkeley. I knew that Berkeley is next to San Francisco, and in my stupid mind San Francisco was a suburb of Los Angeles. That's what I thought. You see, this idiotic idea that America is small was very strong in my mind. In school I had an atlas and in the atlas Hungary had been in the middle and filled a page; the United States was a quarter of a page—of course on an entirely different scale but this I never looked at—and I somehow thought, 'Yes, America is somehow far away and big but it cannot be so very big.'

"So I went and bought at an auction in Brooklyn a 1917 Dodge, got some retread tires for it, and decided to go across the Continent by car. I started out from New York and everything went well until Ohio. In Ohio I turned over with the car; I got on a freshly-tarred road and the car skidded, and I turned over in a field, but luckily nothing serious happened to the car, except that a windshield broke. When farmers nearby helped me to turn the car back on its wheels, it settled with a thud, and when I stepped on the starter, it started without any trouble.

"So I went farther, and it took me one solid month to arrive in California, with an infinite amount of grief as I had very bad tires and a great amount of tire repair, but nevertheless I did arrive. I found out rather fast that if I was to take the appointment I couldn't commute 500 miles between motion pictures and the University. So I left San Francisco and went to Los Angeles, where I had the address of a doctor which somebody gave me, at the Los Angeles General Hospital. I told him that I was looking for some place here, and he said, 'Well, you don't want to come to the General Hospital. The pay is bad; it's awful hours,' and all this. 'You did laboratory work, didn't you?' I said, 'Yes.' 'Well, I have an acquaintance, a certain Dr. Terry, who has a clinical laboratory and I know that he is looking for somebody to help him.'

"I went over to this lab. It was a commercial clinical lab. I met Dr. Terry and we liked each other, and I decided that I would work for him. And after two days I found out that I could be there for 10 million years and would never earn a penny,

26

because Dr. Terry was a fussbudget. I don't mean this in a bad way, but he himself was almost hungry. He made every examination 15 times to be sure. Also he had a very small circle of doctors who sent patients to him. I told him that I would try to do some promotion for his lab. I had some visiting cards printed, saying carefully, 'formerly of the Rockefeller Institute.' Then I went and visited in that same building some 30 doctors and asked them to send us material, promising that we did fast work. The lab started to flower like anything. I think two months later we cleared some $3,000, when the normal total intake of Terry was about $400 a month. Terry was happy and I would have been happy, except for one thing. I was there in the morning at 7 and until late in the evening, doing Wassermans, hemoglobin counts, all the routine jobs, and I'd never seen a studio, not even from the outside.

"I spent one more month there and then I told Dr. Terry, 'I'm sorry I can't stay,' and I got out in the fresh air and walked over to see the studios—the outside. To get in was utterly impossible. Everywhere stood a policeman with a gun, and unless you had an appointment with somebody which was verified by phone, you couldn't get in. Then came days and days of nothing but walking the streets and daydreaming and thinking. And in between, the money that I had started with got lower and lower, and some months later, one beautiful day, I found myself without any money. I was only able to pay my rent and nothing more. I knew that I could not stay at this place without paying rent, so I moved out to an orange grove between Pasadena and Hollywood, which I decided not only to trespass upon but to take as mine. I selected a part where I could sit comfortably and could sleep at night; I had cover there. That's just the truth: I was a bum who lived in an orange grove, eating the owner's oranges. Every day or every second day I walked out on the highway and thumbed a ride to Hollywood.*

*During this period Paul somehow managed to write some stories for Western pictures (the formula was not hard to capture!) and to direct Lucille LaVerne in a production of Ibsen's *Ghosts*, at the Egan Theatre in Los Angeles. Otherwise he was unemployed, unless one counts some forays into professional boxing, where he got five dollars for every round he lasted—plus cauliflower ears which were with him as long as he lived.

"One day I saw a car coming—it was a big Pierce Arrow—and I hesitated to try to make the sign to get a lift, because I didn't think it would pick me up. But there was only one man in it, and I made the motion, and he came to a stop. I walked over and said, 'Thank you,' and stepped in. He said, 'Where are you going?' I said, 'Hollywood.' He said, 'Fine. I'm going there, too.' And then we started to talk, the two of us; first weather and all the small talk.

"He asked me what I was doing in Hollywood. I said, 'Nothing. I'm looking for a possibility, looking for a break.' 'What sort of break?' I confessed to him that I wanted to be a director. In turn, he got confidential and confessed to me that he wanted to be a producer. Then after a while he asked me if I would eat dinner at his house. I said, 'Thank you'; it meant food. I went over—he lived in Hollywood Hills— and had dinner with him, and during dinner he talked about his ambitions and ideas of being a producer, and I talked about directing. Most of the talk was an iconoclastic knocking-down of everything which existed in Hollywood. I also told him about my experience in Hungary.

"When the dinner was over—I didn't know the name of the gentleman—he turned to me and said, 'How much money would you need to make a picture?' I said, 'Any money. It doesn't make any difference how much it is. I can make a picture from any money.'

"Then he said, 'Well, what would you do?' I said, 'I would make a picture which would be timeless.' 'What does that mean?' I tried to explain that the motion picture does not use one of its greatest assets, and that is that one can be, regardless of time and space, anywhere, and that the jump in time or in space can be made without pain for the audience. So one can designate loss of time by a candle which burns down, and so on. I told him I wanted to make a film this way. I also told him that I would like to make a story which had happened during an impossibly short time. He said, 'How short?' I said, 'A second, a fraction of a second.'

"He looked at me and said, 'You are either crazy or you're a genius!' We talked about this further, and then suddenly he got up, walked into the next room, and came back from the room

28

with a little piece of paper in his hand, walked over to me and said, 'This is a check for $5,000. This is all the money I have. Or rather, I have a thousand dollars more which will keep us alive while you make the picture. Here is the money.' And he handed the check over to me. Only then did I see the name which was signed under it; it was Edward M. Spitz.

"Later I found out he was the son of the owner of the Quackenbush Department Stores in New Jersey, and he desperately wanted to break into movies. His father gave him $10,000 to get it out of his system, and this $5,000 plus $1,000 was the remnant of this.

"I finally understood that he really meant it; that the money was mine, and that I should get busy next morning. So next morning I went to an agent whom I had known and asked him if he had some young actors or actresses who were desperately wanting to go ahead but couldn't get a break. He had. 'Well,' I said, 'Look. I have some money to make a picture. I would use these kids but I can't pay them. If they're willing to come into this production on the understanding that after the picture is finished and I get money I will pay them, I will be happy to use them.' He gave me his list and marked the people he thought were potentials, and I promised to look them up.

"Then I set out in search of a leading lady. I had seen a picture of Chaplin in 1923, called *The Gold Rush*, and in it was a woman by the name of Georgia Hale, who was very attractive and seemed a good actress. I had seen her in a sort of soap-opera-heartbreaking role, in which she was very good and not soap-opera like, and I decided that if ever I made a picture this woman must be in it. Now came the quest to go after Georgia Hale and get her for the picture.

"Georgia Hale was riding high. She was, just after Chaplin's picture, under contract to Paramount, and the chances to get her, I knew, were one in a million. Nevertheless, I decided to go after it, and from an acquaintance of mine, who was an assistant director at Paramount, I found out when and where she would be on location. The location was the Paramount ranch right next to Hollywood, where they did most of their exteriors.

"I went out there and found her unit. I waited until they finished and the director called lunch, and then when she sat down to eat lunch and her maid brought a lunchbox and opened it up, I walked over and told her, 'Miss Hale, I don't know you, but I would like to speak to you for five minutes.' Very coolly, she looked at me and said, 'About what?' I said, 'About a role.' 'What role?' I said, 'In a picture that I will make.' 'What studio?' I said, 'I don't know.' 'How come?' I said, 'It's an independent picture. I will rent studio space.'

"She said, 'Well, if it is about a role, you will see my agent.' I said, 'I will not see your agent, Miss Hale, I want to talk to you.' 'Why not?' I said, 'Because I want you to work for me for nothing.' She looked at me and started to laugh like anything and said, 'You must be crazy. Get away from me or I'll call the police.' I said, 'Look, there is no policeman on this set. It will take you half an hour to get a policeman. The policeman can't do anything to me because I'm not trying to get fresh. I really and truly believe that you are the only woman who can play this.'

"Finally, I think in order to get rid of me, she said, 'All right. Tell me the story.' And I was still standing. She didn't ask me to sit down. I started to tell her the story and about what her part called for. She listened to it, without interruption, and when it was all over she said, 'Well, if at the time you shoot this I am not working, I'll do it. But you must pay my maid.' I said, 'What does your maid get?' She told me, 'The maid gets $75 a week.' I said, 'I am sorry, that's out. I don't have the money.'

"To cut a long story short, she consented to work, with the proviso that she would only work on days when she was free, at no other time, which I said was all right. And then through this same agent I got a leading man, Otto Mattiesen, who was a young and very talented actor but didn't seem to be able to get anywhere. So I had a leading lady and a leading man. Now, I needed studio space.

"I went over to the Fine Arts Studio, which was a rental studio. It was not a studio like Paramount or Metro, which made their own pictures. This studio rented space to anybody who wanted to come there. I went in and saw the general manager, a gentleman by the name of Freedman, and told him that I would like to rent studio space. He said, 'That's simple. Here is the list,' and he handed me over a list. Studio rent per day was then $500, and half-rent for set-building time. I said to him, 'This is not what I want. I want to rent your studio by the clock, by the hour or by the minute.' He said, 'You must be crazy. You can't work and rent it by the hour. It takes days to build a set.' I said, 'I want to work in a studio when somebody goes off the set. I will use the set that is there.' 'Well, how do you know what sets will be up?' I said, 'It doesn't make any difference what set is up. I'll go into it when your people go out and I'll pay the pro-rata of the $500.'

"He looked at me and said, 'Are you drunk?' I said, 'No, I am not.' After about half an hour of talk, he said, 'All right. You may pay so much per minute'—I don't remember what it came to.

"Now, I needed raw material. You see, the $5,000 was much too insufficient because then a normal picture, on an average, cost about $200,000 to $250,000. It was to be a full feature— 6 reels. I had no script—only in my head—which I shall explain shortly.

"So I needed raw film material, and luckily for me at that time DuPont decided to break into motion pictures. Up to that time all the raw film had been supplied by Kodak or Agfa. No-body used DuPont in Hollywood. I went to the representative of DuPont and told him that here was a chance. 'Give me film on credit and I'll feature DuPont at the beginning, feature DuPont at the end, and all that.' He consented and I got I don't know how many thousand feet for nothing, sort of on-the-cuff.

"Then I needed a cameraman. I had known several of them and knew one, a very good young one, who also didn't get the breaks and always got very small pictures to shoot. I went to him. His name was Leon Shamroy. He is now an Oscar winner many times. I went to Leon and asked him if he would gamble with me and shoot the picture, and he said yes, but we still needed a camera. Leon was able to rent one on credit.

"Then I started working. And here was the reason for the absence of a script. I decided to make a picture on that old popular hypothesis that anybody who is in live danger, knowingly in live danger, at the last moment of his life sees his whole life in front of him like a kaleidoscope. The trick was that I wanted to make this picture so that when the audience saw it they really would believe that it was happening in the fraction of a second. And to some extent, I succeeded.

"I started to shoot the picture and I finished it in about two and a half to three months. During this time there were sometimes days when I couldn't work; sometimes I worked hard all day, and I worked always in a set which somebody had just left. I went into the Fine Arts every day and looked at the sets that were being built. In one corner there would be the Monte Carlo gambling casino—I just wrote it down and went home. In another place they built a hospital corridor—I wrote it down. And then I simply took the life of my hero and matched it to the sets. So whatever happened to him, I had the set ready for it.

"It was impossible to coordinate the availability of the set with the availability of the actors and actresses. Hale appeared in the picture altogether only a short time, herself. But another woman, whom I used as double, appeared during the rest of the time. What I did, wherever it was possible, when I didn't have the principals, was to photograph hands and feet and objects.* So, for instance, Georgia Hale married my hero, lived with the hero for five years; then the marriage went sour and they divorced. This on the film took a very short time, for what I had done was to photograph Hale full when I had her one day in a hospital set, holding the hand of my hero—she was a nurse. Then I photographed a page of the hospital record where it was written that 'The recovery of the man was uneventful. He was discharged.' Then I showed him coming out of the hospital, then I dissolved into a park, showing a bench from the rear, because I didn't have either the leading man or the leading lady, and I myself had a hand around the imaginary leading lady—the face was not visible—and then I pulled her down and gave her a very deep kiss. This ran into two hands in front of a jeweler's tray, selecting a wedding ring. Then came bells which were ringing, which I shot at San Juan Capistrano, at the Mission. Then came an organist's hand on an organ with Lohengrin's 'Wedding March' on the music rack. And then came a cage, a bird cage, in which were

*For which device Paul received great critical credit for artistry.

32

two white doves cooing; the two white doves suddenly dissolved into two black crows biting each other—the marriage was breaking up—and then there was a shot, if I remember, of a bedroom and a bed, with just two heads—you couldn't see who they were —and the man reached over and yanked the pillow away from the woman. Then came a dirty kitchen sink piled up with dishes. So there were all sorts of symbolic shots, suggesting that the marriage had gone on the rocks. Then came a hand holding a gavel, hitting down with it, and then came an interlocutory decree. I mean, this was in seconds, and it meant five years. And the whole film was made this way. The aim was to make it in kaleidoscope-like speed, as it might seem in actuality to the hero when he was dying. It was called *The Last Moment.*

"So we had the film ready. Also the laboratory I got on credit, but that's usual. And then I sat down with Leo and said, 'What do we do now?' I said, 'Do you think it's good?' Leo said, 'It's marvelous.' I said, 'Yes, you say it, I say it, but we don't know.' So we decided to get the toughest critic from Hollywood to come and see the picture. At that time this was Mr. Welford Beaton, who had then a paper of his own called *Film Spectator*. I called him up one afternoon and told him that he would not know me but I was an independent director and had just made a picture which I was very anxious to show him. He said, 'Why me?' I said, 'Because you are the toughest critic around and I really would like to know if the picture is good or bad.' He said, 'Well, all right, have it at the Telox Laboratories tomorrow afternoon at 3 o'clock and I will look at it.'

"I said, 'I'm sorry, Mr. Beaton, I can't do that.' He said, 'Why?' I said, 'Because I have no credit there and I have no money to pay for the projection. If you come over to the Fine Arts then I can project, for there it doesn't cost me anything.' 'When at the Fine Arts? Tomorrow afternoon at three?' I said, 'No, it must be after 6 o'clock because only then is the projection room free. The rest of the time there are paid people there.' He said he would come.

"I decided to call up another tough critic, Tamar Lane of *Film Mercury*. And in due course, the next evening, both of them arrived and we started to project the picture. Leo, the cameraman,

33

was up in the booth doing the projection; I sat in the room with the others, but away from them, letting them talk as they wanted. I looked to the front every time a reel was changed, hoping to see some sign from them: did they like it or didn't they? They didn't move. When the first reel was over, Leo ran down and asked me, 'How is it?' I said, 'I don't know.' Finally the picture ended; there was no sign from the front; both of them got up and walked to the back where I sat at a console table.

"Then Welford Beaton turned to me and said, 'Who directed that picture?' I said, 'I did.' He had his hat on, which was customary in a projection room in Hollywood. He took his hat off. He very ceremoniously turned to me and said, 'Sir, I am in humble obeisance in front of you. It is the greatest motion picture I have ever seen!' And I thought, 'He's being sarcastic,' and I had my fist clenched to hit him, and I thought, 'Does he know how much I suffered for this picture?' But then he spoke further and I saw that he really meant it. And then Tamar Lane said, 'I am writing a critique on this, in the next *Film Mercury*, in a box,' (which was again a great honor, that the critique was boxed, not just straight).

"Three days later both of them—the *Mercury* and the *Spectator*—came out with a terrific criticism about the picture. I mean, it had all the praise under the sun. I'm ashamed to recall the things which were in them.

"When the papers came out in the evening, I went with Leo on Hollywood Boulevard and saw everywhere the headlines and all, but neither of us had a penny to be able to buy a dinner.

"Then two days later, late at night, the watchman at Fine Arts came over to me and shook me up. (During this whole picture I lived at the Fine Arts Studio, on the sets, selecting always a bedroom set where I could sleep, and I slept on everything from enormous, elaborate royal beds to little jail beds.) The watchman came and shook me and said, 'You're wanted on the phone.' A phone call at this time of the morning—it was three o'clock!

"I went over to the phone—it was Mr. Beaton, who said to me, 'I am at Mr. Chaplin's house. I've just seen his last picture, and I told him it's a very good picture, but it's not as good as the one I saw of yours. Mr. Chaplin wants to see your picture immediately. Could you send it out to his house?'

"Well, it was three o'clock in the morning. I didn't own a car, I didn't have any money for a taxi, and Chaplin lived in Beverly Hills, I don't know how many miles from the studio, but I said, 'Yes, I will get the picture over, but it will take a little time.' I went over to the projection room and grabbed out the big iron box, which weighed, oh, 50 or 60 pounds, put it on my shoulder and started out toward Beverly Hills. It was an awfully long walk. Luckily when I got to the Beverly Theater I saw a milk truck; the driver gave me a lift, and I went over to Chaplin's place.

"There a butler opened the door. I told him that this is the picture which Mr. Chaplin wished to see. He took it away from me and slammed the door, and away I went not knowing what happened.

"That afternoon I tried to phone Beaton to find out what Chaplin had said. I couldn't get him. But the next evening I had the picture previewed in the Beverly Theater—that was through the connection with Tamar Lane; he told them that this was an extraordinary picture, and they should put it on.

"I sat inside during the time the picture was on, and then I ran out—I wanted to be outside to hear what the people would say when they came out. Everybody under the sun was there. Finally I saw Chaplin coming out, with four men on one side and four men on the other, and Chaplin stopped in front of the door and said, 'Well, didn't I tell you that he's a genius!' The 'he' was I.

"But in spite of all that, I went to bed without dinner. The next morning the mad rush started. I got one call after the other from agents who all wanted to sign me up. I signed up with Lichtig and Englander, because old man Lichtig was the one who got me all the actors for nothing, not all but most of them for nothing. Previously he had been the one who had tried to talk me out of this insanity. He had tried to explain to me, 'You have $5,000. It's not enough for any big picture, but you can make a little Western out of it, why don't you make that? Why this big thing? You'll fail in it.' Well, I didn't follow the advice, and *The Last Moment* did not fail.

"United Artists took over *The Last Moment* for release. The preview in the Beverly Theater had been in November 1927. On March 12, 1928 the picture was premiered in New York."

The critical reception of *The Last Moment* is worth looking at. Welford Beaton, in *The Film Spectator* of Nov. 26, 1927, began with the headline: "INTRODUCING YOU TO MR. PAUL FEJOS, GENIUS." He continued for a full page in that vein. "Paul Fejos is a name that you probably never heard before. But you will hear it again. Fejos is an extraordinary picture genius . . . [He] is the hero of the production. . . . If the plan for a motion picture hall of fame goes through, I hereby nominate for a large niche Paul Fejos. He has won his right to immortality, even if he never makes another picture."

The National Board of Review Magazine (February 1928) said: "Nothing quite like this film has ever been done before. . . . The method allows the medium to hold sway in a technical virtuosity. This manipulation of pattern and image, light and shadow, in a constant shifting and convolution, is of itself enough to cast an enthralling spell. The pictures alone count—or rather the *moving* pictures. In short, it is cinema on its own, distinct, like painting, poetry, music. The medium is permitted to achieve its own results."

When *The Last Moment* opened the next March in New York at the Greenwich Village Theater, the *New York Times* called it "a remarkable picture . . . infinitely more absorbing than many pictures on which twenty times the amount has been expended . . . Dr. Fejos, who has devoted years to stage designing and direction, as well as medicine, reveals a wonderful aptitude for true cinematic ideas. He has succeeded in telling this story with one title and a few written or printed inserts."*

*In none of his silent pictures did Paul use subtitles to any extent. Murneau's *The Last Laugh* (1925), with Emil Jannings, had been the first introduction, to Americans, of titleless narration. Murneau probably had some influence on Paul.

Because *The Last Moment* was the product of an independent studio, diligent searching has not resulted in finding a copy of the film.

36

All the critics noted (1) that Paul Fejos was a Hungarian, (2) that he was a doctor of medicine and a bacteriologist, and (3) that the picture had been produced on less than a shoestring budget.

The Last Moment was named as one of the ten best pictures of the year, and was voted the honor film of 1928 by the National Board of Review.

"Then my agent, Harry Lichtig, took me every day to a different studio. All the studios called for me, and from every studio I walked out. The walking out was partly because I was frightfully young and partly because I had certain ideas of what I wanted, which didn't jell with any of the studios. I wanted absolute discretion on selection of story, absolute discretion on casting; only I and nobody else should see the rushes, and only I cut the picture. And this, of course, they didn't want to touch. I went to studio after studio, Paramount, Fox, Twentieth Century, Warner's, just to walk out in the middle of the conferences.

"Then finally, one day Harry called me up and said that I was due for an appointment at 11:30 at Universal to see Carl Laemmle, the owner of Universal. I said to Harry, 'I don't think so, Harry. Universal is a lousy outfit. I wouldn't fit there.' He said, 'Listen, Paul, you have been in every studio; you've turned down every studio in Hollywood. There is no other place.' So I went over to Universal, where I saw Uncle Carl, Carl Laemmle. He was a very congenial old man, a German, who was a cloak-and-suit man before he went to Hollywood. He was very kind and very sweet, which I was reluctant to admit, because I saw in every producer only an enemy. He told me that they had asked me to come there because his son, Carl Laemmle, Jr., had seen the picture and had said he was crazy about it. So, 'I thought we'd give you a contract to make one picture and try you out.' I said, 'What would be the one picture?' He said, 'Well, we are thinking that you could make one of our jewels.' Universal had their pictures rated as 'jewels' and 'super-jewels.'

"And I said, 'What should that be?' He said, 'Well, you would make for us an aviation adventure picture, or possibly a very sexy picture, but I mean a cleanly-sexy picture.' This infuriated me and I said, 'Mr. Laemmle, I am not making aviation pictures and I would not know how to make a clean sexy picture. Harry, let's go.'

"He got up and looked at me with pleading and said, 'Sit back.' I said, 'No, Harry, let's go, it's useless. We are taking the time of Mr. Laemmle for nothing.'

"Then the door opened—there's always a door opening which decides things—and in walked a young boy. He was then 17 years old, Carl Laemmle, Jr. He was the apple of his father's eye and anything he wanted, his father would do for him. When he was 18 years old, he became general manager of the entire Universal Pictures, a many-million-dollar enterprise. So Junior walked in, walked over and said to me, 'I've seen *The Last Moment*; it was fantastic!' and this and that. 'Did you sign a contract with my Dad?' I said, 'No, I didn't.' 'Why not?' I said, 'Well, Mr. Laemmle offered to have me make one of his jewels and he wants an aviation adventure or a clean sexy picture, and I didn't think I could do it.'

"So Junior walked over to the desk of the old man—he just said, 'Papa, you promised me! You don't understand anything about this. You're old'—and I don't know what—'cruel.' He turned to me and said, 'Please have lunch with us. We must talk about this more.'

"We went out to the Universal commissary with old man Laemmle and young Laemmle and had lunch there, and during lunchtime Junior talked to me and told me that I could have anything I wanted at the studio, with the proviso that any picture I would make must be a Carl Laemmle, Jr., production. I said, 'It's yours.'

"He said, 'Now about the money.' I said, 'I don't give a damn about the money; as long as I can do the pictures I want, that's all I care for.' I signed a contract that afternoon for five years, with six-month options, with Universal and went to work for them.

"They had at the story-department properties—that's what they called them—stories that they owned, and naturally the first order of business was that I should get all the stories and read them and select one of them, because they'd rather use something they had than buy a new one. So I sat there on 'director's row,' which was called 'pneumonia row' because everybody got pneumonia there, it was so drafty, and read scripts from morning until midnight. Nothing! It was the most horrible amount of balderdash that I ever read; each one was worse than the other. Most of them were stolen from classics and very badly adapted, with names changed and age changed and all that, but everywhere the thing stuck out. I couldn't find a single story.

"I had no preconceived ideas about what I wanted to do, but I wanted to do something new. I wanted to do something new in technique or new in feeling. And they had nothing.

"Finally I went back to the story department and said, 'You can take back all the stories, I don't want any of them. Don't you have anything else?' They said they had some material but I wouldn't be interested because this was for shorts, short subjects. I said, 'Let me see them,' and took them down to my office and read them, and among them I came across a title called *Lonesome*. It was a very small script, three pages, the outline of it. It was about a girl and a boy in New York City, who have no friends and who are utterly lonesome. And these two people on a Sunday, as they have nothing to do and they have no friends, start out separately to Coney Island to spend the afternoon there. At Coney Island they meet accidentally and fall in love. Then some circumstance separates the two and neither of them knows the other's name, and there starts a desperate search at Coney Island from roller coaster to merry-go-round to try to find each other, but they don't. At the very end of the picture—a happy ending—they find each other. But it was poignantly-written, a beautiful, lovely, tiny little gem.

"I ran with it to Junior and said, 'This is what I want to make!' Junior called up the story department and told them that I had selected this, and there was a lengthy talk on the phone. Junior said, 'Well, well,' and didn't say anything to me. Then, finally, when he put down the receiver, he said, 'They're all against it. They say it's a property that they bought for $25 and it's silly, and it's nothing, it's a travelogue.'

" 'Well,' I said, 'travelogue or not, that's what I want to make and my contract says *I* select the story.' Junior said, 'All right.'

Then I needed to cast it and, of course, they told me to go through all the people whom Universal had under contract first, before I selected somebody from the outside. I selected a very young, 17-year-old British and Canadian girl for the female lead, and one of Universal's very bright boys, sort of a wise-cracking, semi-comedian, Glenn Tryon, for the boy. The girl's name was Barbara Kent. Tryon was very popular.

"On of the reasons I selected the story was that it reminded me of New York. I wanted to put in a picture New York with its terrible pulsebeat, everybody rushing; where even when you have time, you run down to the subway, get the express and then change over to a local, and all these things; this terrific pressure which is on people, the multitude in which you are always moving but you are still alone, you don't know who is your next neighbor. There was, by the way, an O. Henry twist in *Lonesome*: at the very end the boy and girl found out that they lived side-by-side in the same rooming house, but they had never known about each other. It sounds corny, but let's say that it was high corn.

"So that was the first picture I made for Universal. It was received very well. Laemmle, Sr., was crying so at the projection. His secretary needed to go out to get a new handkerchief. It was a tear-jerker."

This was also in 1928. It was more than a tear-jerker. The picture is still shown in France each year as an example of a good story told with what were then very advanced cinema techniques in the use of crowds and in rapid montage effects which made full use of the medium for an emotional impact. It dates much less, when seen today, than most pictures of its vintage.

The National Board of Review Magazine (August 1928) said of *Lonesome* when it was released:

"[It] makes you see that the motion picture can be important when dealing with supposedly simple things, that it can always make them interesting, and that it needs no chariot races and no great spectacles. The need is to be cinematic. Dr. Fejos recognizes this necessity first of all, and his aim to meet it is constant."

"Then in 1928 I made a picture—may the Lord forgive it—which was called *Eric the Great*. It was with Conrad Veidt, the German star. Mary Philbin was the leading woman. This was a story of a magician and a tale of jealousy and a tricky murder arising out of the jealousy. So, as you see, I was going toward Hollywood already. But Conrad Veidt was a grand actor and it was fun to work with him.

"That one was followed by another picture called *Captain of the Guard*, which was about the French Revolution. This was with John Bowles and Laura La Plante. This was still silent.

"In 1928, too, *Lonesome* was called back from New York and I was asked to make some talking sequences for it, because talking films were already in. Universal wanted to relase it as a partly talking picture, so they recorded an entire musical background and about five or six sets of dialogues. It was sheer horror, but then no picture could go which was entirely silent.

"Then they decided that I should make the most expensive property that Universal ever had. That was Philip Dunning's and George Abbot's *Broadway*, which seemed a very unfortunate proposition for Universal because it cost them as a silent version half a million dollars, and they spent another half a million to buy the talking rights. So there was a picture the rights for which cost a million dollars and I had the extreme and doubtful honor to make it. And I didn't know what the hell to do with it! *Broadway* is a very good play, but the whole thing happened in a tiny little back room in a nightclub, and outside of five main characters, nobody else was in it. Nothing big was happening. It was the intimate story of gangsters and entertainers. I was in a heck of a dilemma.

"And Junior came to me and told me that my budget was five million dollars! I couldn't see where five million dollars could be put in the picture and told him so. He said, 'Oh, you will spend the money.' I said, 'Junior, I can't. I mean, the cast is all together 12 people, there are only three stars in it, there's one set. What will we do?'

"Finally one of Junior's advisers, I don't know which one, gave him the very bright idea that *Broadway* must stand on its own production value. This meant that the money spent on it must show. So we built a nightclub set which was bigger, literally, than Grand Central Station. The nightclub was so big that when I worked on the full set the rest of the studio couldn't work because it had no electricity; I needed it all, just for this one set. The tragedy was, however, that in this horrible abortion, this dreadful big nightclub, the Paradise Club, Glenn Tryon, who played a small hoofer, was constantly dreaming about 'big time.' He was in a nightclub which was bigger than anything that was ever built, and he was there dreaming of the big time. Anyhow, the picture was made. Paul Porcasi was the nightclub owner; Evelyn Brent and Merna Kennedy were also in it. Also Glenn Tryon.

"It was one of the saddest works I'd ever made in my life. I had extras galore, so that I didn't know what to do with them. Hundreds of extras were needed to make the nightclub somewhat full. It was a horror! But I succeeded in spending the five million dollars and finished the picture in 1929. And it was a success. Universal earned a lot of money on it. I was not happy about it and I was not proud."

Paul's technical ingenuity was always part of his total artistry. For *Broadway* he and his cameraman, Hal Mohr, invented an overhead steel camera crane weighing 28 tons and mounted on a six-wheel truck chassis. It could pivot and swirl and swoop, and could make musical dance numbers seem like something from another world. It has been said that no film did more to restore mobility to the sound camera, and that the development of this crane has become something of a camera legend. "Today, the dramatic aspects of *Broadway* seem mannered and fairly silly, but the images of the Paradise [Club] and the huge musical numbers (the finale in Technicolor), have become basic screen literature."* But *Broadway* was the beginning of his disillusion with Hollywood. A subsequent event made him bitter about Universal.

*Miles Kreuger: *Manuscript of The American Musical Film.* Quoted in release by the Museum of Modern Art Department of Film, on "The Roots of the American Musical Film (1927-32)," 1971.

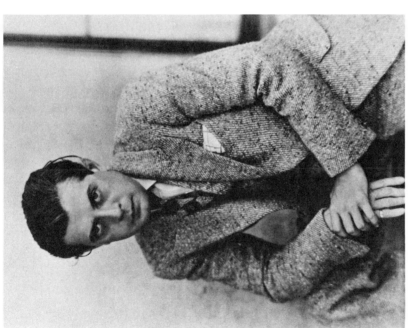

The first camera crane used by Paul for Broadway, 1929

Paul in Hollywood about 1929

43

"Universal bought at that time, at my instigation, a book, a German book, *All Quiet on the Western Front*. I had read it in the German and went nuts about it. I ran to Junior, 'Please buy it.' And they bought the book for 500 miserable dollars, which was immensely cheap because most properties then cost $10,000, $20,000, $30,000.

"So they bought this and I looked forward to making it. The First World War was something I knew firsthand, and I felt that I could really do something with it. I took it for granted that I would make the picture. To my greatest surprise, a week later, I was called into Junior's office and Junior told me that he had made the biggest coup of his life: 'I have contracted Paul Whiteman.' I said, 'So what?' 'Oh, you don't understand. You're not an American. Paul Whiteman is the king of jazz; it's the most well-known name in America, and we will have him for a picture.' I said, 'Junior, what will you do with him? He's a man inordinately fat. I don't think you can hang a love interest on him. He didn't have a career which included shooting anybody; he nicely advanced higher and higher and became a very fine jazz conductor. But what on earth will you do with him?' Nothing doing —'We must get a story for him.' So I said, 'All right, get the story.'

"On all the lots of Universal, the 30 writers in the story department tried to write a story, to write one picture. Each was worse than the other. All of them falsified the figure, and all of them were terrible. Then Junior talked big, called the story department, and said, 'Send to each of the great writers in America a cable or a wire that we want them to write a story on Whiteman, and send it that way, with '100-word answer paid.'

"The first answer that came back was from Paris, from Theodore Dreiser, who wired 100 times the words, 'no, never, no, never, no, never.' Several of the wires were equally sarcastic and nasty, so we couldn't get the thing done by outside writers.

"Then Junior decided: let's contract the man who later married Helen Hayes, Charles MacArthur. And Charlie MacArthur was duly contracted, came to my office and sat there day-in and day-out and told me day-in and day-out, 'You can't do anything with this.' And then finally after five months he gave it up and walked out.

"Meanwhile the starting-time of Whiteman's contract was coming closer and closer; I think he got either $80,000 or $100,000 per week. That included the band. And, of course, the band was the worst trouble because it meant that it must always be on hand and you can't have it for love scenes and this scene and that scene. We didn't know what the hell to do with it.

"Finally it was decided to make a revue out of it, a tremendous big color revue; production value: seven million dollars! So for the second time I stood before a beautiful proposition, seven million dollars. Wherever we could spend money we tried desperately to do it. When the girl came over to me to okay some dresses, I would always say, 'It's too cheap. Back. Get some others.'

"I remember we had a bridal number in it, in which a girl walked up a long stairway to Whiteman's music and had a veil which was 110 feet long. It was Brussels lace. Just to spend the money somehow, because we didn't know what to do. This was very typical of Hollywood at this point.

"I didn't want to do the picture, but I didn't dare to say, 'I refuse to do it,' which would have been the proper thing to do. Its title was *The King of Jazz*; it was released in 1930. When it was over, everybody was supremely happy. The Whiteman Orchestra was so happy that when they left they sent me a gold cigarette case to tell how pleased they were they were out of it.

"When that was over, I had my belly full and finally went over to Junior and said, 'It doesn't go anymore.' I accused him of breaking the contract, that they made me make a picture I didn't want to make.' He said, 'But it was a great success.' I said, 'Success for you, but not for me.' And I just decided to break the contract and get out. Lewis Milestone had directed *All Quiet on the Western Front*.

"I was completely empty and messed up. I had plenty of money, but that was about all that existed. So I went into Junior's office and told him I was quitting. Junior screamed, 'You can't quit. We'll put you on the blacklist!' I finally went into the office of the old man, Laemmle, Sr., who listened to me and turned to Junior and said, 'Look, if the doctor is unhappy, let him go. It's no use to have an unhappy man.'

"And I said, 'You are right, I couldn't make pictures here no matter what.' So I left Universal and for about three months I was on the blacklist. My agent came to me and told me, 'No studio wants to touch you. Universal put the mark on you.'*

"In all decency to Laemmle, Jr.,—he was always a good friend of mine—I must say that he sent the equivalent of my check every single week over to my house, so that I should not be in trouble.

"Then three months later I signed a contract with Metro-Goldwyn-Mayer, which was then *the* studio, at the top, not in art but at least in intelligence. I started working there, and the first picture I made was a picture which already existed in English called *The Big House*. This was the story of a prison riot in San Quentin, and I needed to make this in German and in French. Possibly the only interesting thing in it was that I imported for *The Big House* an actor who afterwards became quite a potentate in Hollywood—Charles Boyer.

"When I finished this, I suddenly started to ask myself, 'What am I doing in Hollywood? This is not what I want. What I am doing is silly, is aimless, has no real value,' and somehow—let's put it that way—I had fallen out of love with Hollywood. And in 1931, I decided to go back to Europe. The decision happened in a second. I was sitting in my office at the studio and some terribly stupid inter-office memo was on my desk, which made me very angry. It was something from the story department; they wanted this or wanted that. I got very angry and called my secretary and said, 'Pack all my private correspondence, and call Miss Newcomb when I've left and tell her that she should tell

---

*As a matter of fact, the sequence of events here is a little confusing. It was publicly announced that *The King of Jazz* was to be a Paul Fejos production, but the film was ultimately given to another director, John Murray Anderson—a Broadway director with no film background. It may well be that Paul did walk out on this picture (at what stage it is not clear). At any rate he did break his contract and was briefly blacklisted. He always carried the gold cigarette case engraved with the names of the members of the Whiteman orchestra; the gift had made him very happy.

The arrival of Paul Whiteman to make The King of Jazz, *1929. Left to right: Carl Laemmle, Jr., Whiteman, Carl Laemmle, Sr., Paul Fejos.*

Albert Einstein and Paul (right) on set of The Big House, *1930.*

47

Irving Thalberg that I left for Europe and 'Good-bye, thanks for the buggy ride.'

"Two hours later I was on the 'Chief' going to Chicago and New York. I stayed in New York for three days, looked at some theater, then boarded the old *France* and went over to Paris.

"I simply didn't fit into the Hollywood picture. I found Hollywood phony, not just the people but the city itself; it's a reclaimed desert and artificial. I found everything artificial. I found the people impossible; I mean, for example, the people in the story departments; writers, so-called writers, utterly unintelligent, utterly uneducated, stupid hacks, who sat down in afternoons in an office for story conferences and tried to build a drama. It was always built the same way: they all had these little Hollywood story books in which things are written up as clues: mistaken identity, parental intereference, and I don't know what. And from that you build up a thing. It was just impossible to stand."

Thus Paul Fejos and Hollywood in the late 1920s and early 1930s. Those were the "dream factory" years—before Hollywood had learned to manufacture nightmares. Its product was highly standardized, infinitely repetitive and imitative of itself, reflecting a sort of mythology of life in America. In 1930 Warner Brothers produced *Little Caesar*, and the year 1931 saw the production of 50 gangster films. There were 30-odd *Tarzan* films after the first one in 1918, and they grossed 200 million dollars. Most pictures were a glamorization of life in a fantasy world, lacking the most basic of artistic moralities: truth to life—the dramatic honesty which can distinguish the counterfeit from the real, which shows a respect for human beings as human beings and does not deal in evasive oversimplifications.

The industry was under the domination of the big studios; the independent producer, so common today, was at that time an anomaly. Some distinguished films were made, to be sure: Von Stroheim's *Greed* (1924), Josef von Sternberg's *Salvation Hunters* (1925), Murneau's *Sunrise* (1927), King Vidor's *The Crowd* (1928). But the first three of these were made by non-Americans. Paul called the *Salvation Hunters* "a fabulously good picture." It was produced independently on a low budget, and was dismissed by all the distributors as something which wouldn't make money. Von Sternberg lost all the money he had put into it. He had a hit in 1928 with Emil Jannings in *The Last Command*. But he really came into prominence by discovering Marlene Dietrich and bringing her to the States. He had directed her in *The Blue Angel* in 1930. So, as Paul used to say, "A gimmick was needed."

Paul's experience in Hollywood was a kind of microcosm of the career of the creative director swimming upstream against the System, who in his early unexpected success confounds that system briefly, but is finally swallowed by its voracious gullet. *The Last Moment* was a sport in the world of cinema, brought to life by the dogged ingenious artistic integrity and creativity of one man (plus, in this instance, a series of lucky accidents). In *Lonesome* Paul was also able to insist upon total control of the process of film-making, and that was again a Hollywood paradox in the twenties. Then, as he makes clear, the system began to surround him, and in his own eyes his artistic stature diminished as his fame grew—grew for the wrong reasons, as he saw it.

Although Paul had come up the hard way in Hollywood, he was there when the European wave of film directors began to be imported by the studios. If "art" could be successful, why not package it in Hollywood? And often the same process of degeneration set in which had embittered Paul: the great directors were given formula stories which defied their artistic talents—to say nothing of what the studios left on the cutting-room floor. And so "art" became not only inartistic: it also proved the worst suspicion of the producers—it failed to pay.

The break with Hollywood, then, was inevitable for Paul, though its manner was as sudden and dramatic as if he had been directing it in one of his own movies.

49

Chapter Three

ADVENTURE BY ACCIDENT

———————————————◆•◆—————————————————

ONCE AGAIN, IN THIS SUDDEN TRANSITION, there was a woman off-screen—or rather on-screen, for Paul had directed Barbara Kent in *Lonesome* in 1928. He had a habit of falling in love with his leading ladies, but Kent was perhaps his first real love after Mara. She was a beautiful young Canadian, a fresh new unknown actress. (Although Paul got older his favorite girls were always young. Kent was seventeen.) Their affair lasted until 1931, the year he left for Europe. It may be that the relationship was diminishing at that time; he wanted Kent to go with him, but she was enchanted by the possibilities of her own career, and refused to go. At any rate, he broke with her and Hollywood at the same time. She married Garbo's agent.

Paul went first to his home surroundings in Hungary. He was greatly depressed, partly perhaps because of Kent, certainly because of his disillusionment with Hollywood and what was happening to his artistic ambitions. He was thinking of killing himself—he had attempted suicide once in Paris with sleeping pills, and was saved only by a doctor friend who found him in time. His moods of despair were always triggered by frustration, by the seeming loss of *control* of the meaning of his life, and suicide seemed one desperate way of maintaining that control.

Just now he was on the edge of such a decision. He was saved from it by a little episode which was completely in character: emotional, dramatic, off-beat, a little fey and other-worldly, mythical in the sense that he was placing himself in his own myth. He decided to play a kind of Russian roulette. He remembered that years before, when he was about ten, in this same little garden in which he now stood, he had hidden a package of chocolate in a tree. He wanted to see if the chocolate was still there, and he made an agreement with himself that if the chocolate *was* still there, he would not kill himself. It was there, bleached white after all these years. "I sat under that tree and I ate it," he said later.

On his return to France in 1931 he negotiated a very favorable contract with a Paris motion-picture studio, Branberger and Richeles, who wanted someone to modernize their studio and to make some films. He directed a film for them called *Fantomas*, and another, *L'Amour Américaine*, with Spinnelly, a famous Parisian actress. He had become an American citizen the preceding year, and so spoke with authority on love in the United States. It was a comedy.

Before he left Hollywood he had purchased from Universal the movie rights to a little Hungarian novel called *Spring Shower*. Back in Hungary again in 1932 he made a movie of this called *Marie, a Hungarian Legend (Légende Hongroise)*, with Annabella in her first starring role. Its story was as simple as that of *Lonesome*, if more mystical and poetic. It was the day of talking-pictures, but only one word, "Marie," was spoken in it. The movie was almost a monodrama—a sort of legendary story about a poor young servant girl in Hungary who is raped, bears a child, dies, and goes to Heaven. Sixteen years later, in earth-time, she looks down on earth and sees her own daughter about to be seduced, as she had been. She seizes a bucket of water and pours it toward earth, inducing a spring shower which saves her daughter.

In Vienna in 1933 he both wrote the story for and directed *Sonnenstrahl*, again with Annabella. There too, the next year, he directed *Frühlingsstimmen*, with the coloratura soprano Adela Kern.

Paris, Budapest, Vienna and then, in 1934, Denmark. Nordisk Films of Copenhagen, like Branberger and Richeles, wanted Paul to modernize their old studios and to direct some films. He made three pictures for Nordisk: *Flight from the Millions (Flugten*

Fra Millionerne), *Prisoner No. 1 (Faenge No. 1)* in 1935, and
The Golden Smile (Den Gyldne Smil) in 1936. Paul was particularly fond of the last one, which told the story of a great actress
who discovers that she has carried her acting so much into her
personal life that she is no longer able to be sincere. Bodil Ipsen
played the actress.

As always, he had been given what he demanded: complete
control of the productions—story selection, casting, directing and
editing. But he was beginning to be bored with studio productions. He found that he simply couldn't work with any pleasure;
as he said, he had no *sitzfleisch*—no perseverance. He had married again in 1936, this time to Inga Arvad, a young starlet and
journalist who had interviewed Hitler. She was a self-confident,
sparklingly handsome blonde. Paul always said that she was an
excellent wife, intelligent and independent and sensible.

He had met Inga while he was directing in Denmark. At one
stage the company was on shipboard and Inga was there. As his
old friend and colleague Lothar Wolff (who was there too)
remembers it, Paul won her attention, and also created some
bewilderment, with a typical Hungarian gesture. Inga had
admired his watch, a complicated mechanism with dates and
stop-mechanism and phases of the moon as well as the time of
day. Paul stripped it from his wrist and held it out to her: "It is
yours." "But what do you mean? I can't take your watch like
this!" Paul persisted; she continued to refuse. Whereupon Paul
took the watch and threw it over the rail into the ocean.

What could she do but marry him?

Everyone who knew Paul was captured by his charm, which
did not depend upon this kind of extravagance. A little under
six feet in height, he was well-proportioned, lithe and graceful.
He had sharp blue eyes and a long upper lip which could twist
at the corners into a kind of whimsical elfin smile, or could turn
grim when he wanted to be grim. He was gracious and urbane.
Always he lived with a deep sense of the comic and the absurd;
he could laugh at himself, a disarming trait. Some of his funniest
stories, which he would act out in your living room, were about
his own predicaments. Perhaps because he had his own sense of
selfhood he could give himself fully in friendship; no one was

ever warmer, more generous, loyal, or understanding with those he liked.*

At this stage Paul had achieved great distinction as a cinema director, but he had reached a kind of personal plateau. He was beginning to be restless. He saw nothing ahead but the making of more movies and somehow the prospect stifled him. All his life he walked out on careers, and women, when he felt he was losing some part of himself that he cherished. He feared being entrapped; his whole search was for freedom of spirit. He was willing to pay the necessary price for that, for it was not always clear what orbit his next mood would take him into. Each new career, however, seemed to encapsulate and make use of all he had assimilated up to that point. More than most people he was a part of all that he had met. Certainly this was true of the apparent about-face he made early in 1936. Here again was a major watershed, and as so often happened with him, it was the result of an accident (more properly a *gesture*) born of an impulse to be free. It sent him to far-off lands he had never thought of visiting, and it deflected his career into anthropology and archeology.

Again the story is best told in his own words:

"One day I walked in on a board meeting of Nordisk Films and told them I want to resign; I wanted my contract cancelled. It had two more years to run, and they refused my request. I said, 'All right, you can refuse it. I am sick, I can't work.' They tried to conciliate me, and Bowder, who was the president, said to me, 'We will do anything for you that you want as long as you continue making pictures.' I told him, 'I'm sorry, I can't make pictures here. I know it now, there's nothing new in it, I just can't stick here anymore.' And he said, 'Well, make pictures somewhere else but make them for us.' I said, 'You wouldn't want to

*At Stanford, Paul would sometimes come into our kitchen and cook a whole Hungarian dinner for us. If we lacked the proper instruments with which to pound the pork, he would rush down to a butcher-supply house and come back with a huge, heavy meat-cleaver (which we still use). Even his self-dramatizing could be both comic and flattering. When we were in San Francisco, he might suggest that we go to Blum's for one of their incredible "Rosebud" ice-cream sundaes. If for any reason my wife demurred, he would as likely as not drop to his knees before her in the sidewalk traffic of Union Square and plead with her to comply. It was difficult to refuse his generosities. J.W.D.

make pictures at the place I want.' He said, 'Where? London? Paris? Of course.' I said, 'No, no, no.' I really had nothing in my mind to say about where I wanted to go, but I just stuck to this, 'No, no, no.'

"In the board room there was a map of the world, and he started to press me, 'Tell us where. We'll finance the picture and you'll make it there.' As I stood there I stood next to Africa and looked on Madagascar, an island which I hardly knew existed. I had heard the name of it but I knew nothing about it; I never read about it; I barely knew where it was. I said, 'The only place I would like to make pictures is Madagascar.' He said, 'But why Madagascar?' I said, 'Because there are native people there and I would like to work with native people.' To my greatest astonishment and great embarrassment, he said, 'All right. Then you go to Madagascar. Which of the cameramen do you want to take?'

"So I selected Fredericksen, and desperately ran to the Copenhagen Public Library to look something up on Madagascar, because I didn't know a damned thing about it. I got two or three books at the library. It was very small pickings, and really didn't tell me anything, but nevertheless in 1936, in April, I boarded a freighter in Bordeaux which went to Madagascar, and I arrived at Tamatave—that's on the east coast—and started to look around at what I could shoot. I was not interested in shooting travelogues of cities or countryside, so I went to the agent of the steamship company and asked him where I could find the most untouched part of Madagascar. He told me it was south, the extreme southern point. It is a mountainous area, parts of which were not then under government control.

"I boarded a very small coastal boat, called the *Norwegian*, and went down to a place where I landed with my cameraman and one more man whom I hired. After about a week's stay I started inland with a caravan. I went first to the fort, which was at Fort-Dauphin, and talked there with the fort commander, who was a young lieutenant in the French colonial army. He painted me dire pictures about my never coming back; the natives were headhunters and cannibals and all that. But I went on in, and found the Tanosi Tribe and the Bara Tribe. For the first time in my life I met primitive natives, and I found them adorable. I found them the most logical people in the world. They were extremely functional, infinitely more so than people in the United States. I found them very clever, far more clever in the way they did things than any of the people I knew in civilized areas. I also found out from them what leisure is, which I had never known really, because leisure up to then only meant to rush more. Even when one is on vacation there are a million things to do that one should do when one is vacationing.

"I shot with the natives thousands of feet of material from which I eventually made several different pictures, shorts, all ethnographic in nature: their ceremonies, their lives.*

"I met with no resistance at all on their part. They were the sweetest people under the sun. Nobody was hostile, but on the other hand, I was not impertinent. I didn't walk into any house where I was not invited, nor did I go near a ceremony they didn't ask me to go near. And that was all that was needed. One of the very great troubles in dealing with primitives is that even the anthropologist with a Ph.D. who goes out among primitive folk sometimes believes that the area is his, and he is an uncrowned king in it. He will shoot game, completely forgetting that the game doesn't belong to him; it belongs to the natives. He doesn't realize that the noise that the gun makes scares the game away and this results in tremendous damage to the native economy.

"I spent six months in Madagascar, at the end of which time a ship was supposed to pick me up at the fort. It was the *Christianafjord* and I got information from my own natives, my runners, from Cap Ste. Marie that they had seen the boat coming. So I packed everything and went down to the bay waiting for the boat to pick me up. The boat came into the bay, arrived at the middle of the bay, suddenly stopped, tooted once, turned around and went out and away. It took me five days to find out from other natives that the boat went northward.

*The films made in Madagascar were: *Dance Contest in Esira*, *The Bilo*, and various other documentary ethnological pictures. *The Bilo* was a superb filming, with sound, of the funeral of a native chief. It included the ceremonial dancing to native music—a dance led by the chief's son—the purpose of which was to put the evil spirits to flight. It also included, though not in full detail, the slaughter at the burial-site of 800 of the chief's oxen. Many of the horns were used to decorate the grave.

"Many months later I found out why. The *Christianafjord* had a contract to call at the Island of Reunion and the Island of Mauritius to pick up cargo, and they came into the bay to pick me up—they didn't know about me, they thought it was only cargo they were after. But when they came into the bay they found it too small and as this was a turbine ship reversing was very difficult, so they decided the hell with it and they would pick up their cargo another time, and they went away.

"This gave me an additional involuntary stay in Madagascar for about three or four months, at the end of which time the small ship which brought me down, the *Norwegian*, came down and picked me up finally. By this time I had also picked up a severe case of malaria. When I got on the boat, the Captain said to me, 'Where do you want to go?' I said, 'I want to go home.' He said, 'Well, you are not going home.' 'Where am I going?' 'Oh,' he said, 'you are going to Africa.' And then I found out that he was going around the island and going to Mozambique, to Chinde, near the mouth of the Zambesi River, which flows into the Indian Ocean.

"So then I stayed on this tiny ship, with the terrible malaria, for about a month until finally it delivered me at the top of Madagascar, Cap d'Ambre, Diego Suarez, where the ship that had deserted me earlier had just put in. It picked me up to take me back to Europe.

"The ship was supposed to make a call at the Seychelles Island group, at Mahé. I went to Mahé with them and got off the ship because I was awfully down with the malaria. The Seychelles were a British crown colony composed of 107 islands and rocks. The main city, if you want to call it a city—there were ten houses —is Mahé. It has a magnificent population: a mixture of African Negroes and Polynesian people—a very beautiful race. I spent three months in Mahé, most of it cruising along the other islands, and then came back on the same kind of boat, a Norwegian freighter, to Copenhagen again.

"I had also made some more films in the Seychelles, and when all this was over I had quite a lot of ethnographic material, including all sorts of specimens: weapons and masks and that sort of thing, which I had collected in Madagascar. The Royal Geographic Society of Denmark asked me if they could present the films I had made. I said, 'Yes,' and one day at one film an elderly gentleman came over to me and asked me if I brought anything back from Madagascar. 'Oh,' I said, 'yes, an awful lot of junk.' Well, he told me that their museum hadn't a single object from Madagascar; could I let them see it and could I give them something? So I gave them a lot of pieces and got acquainted with the elderly gentleman, who was the director of the museum, Dr. Nielsen. He asked me about the different artifacts, what they're used for, the native names of them, who makes them in the tribe, the women or the men, how they are made, and all that.

"And before I knew it, for about two weeks I was talking ethnography to these gentlemen without any education except what I got on the trip. What amazed me was that all the people in the museum accepted me as a colleague and occasionally came over and brought some artifacts from another area and asked me questions about them, areas which I did not know. So I started to read anthropology and ethnology intensively.

"Then in 1937, in January, Swedish Film Industry, which had seen the pictures I had made for Nordisk, the Danish company, sent me an invitation to come to Stockholm at their expense. To cut a long story short, they asked me if I would go out once more on an expedition and make some films for them. Already there were war clouds all over, Munich was on, and all sorts of difficulties. I was somewhat worried about tying myself down now and perhaps not being able to get back to the United States. But the offer was very attractive; they wanted to pay quite a lot of money; they left it up to me to go anywhere I wanted to. I went to old Thomas Thomsen and asked him about what area would be interesting. He was the director of the museum and he was the son of *the* Thomsen, the very early ethnologist. He suggested that I should go to Indonesia and East Asia where they—the museum —needed to know more about the tribes. They also needed artifacts, and thought that if I would go out maybe I could collect some things for them. So I went."

This turned into two long and extensive field trips—to Colombo in Ceylon, Hongkong, Shanghai, Kobe, Yokohama; then

Darien in Korea, the Philippines, then Borneo, Miri, New Guinea, and other parts of what was then the Dutch East Indies: Java, Bali, Lombok, and the Sumbawa Islands. In 1938 he went to Bangkok, still under the aegis of the Swedish Film Industry. Then up to North Siam and then home.

In North Siam, at Chiengmai, he wrote and produced a film called *A Handful of Rice (En Handful Ris)*,* later released also by RKO under the title *The Jungle of Chang*. It was a simple story, told with native "actors," about the rigors of jungle life. It started, as Paul told the story, with a street in Stockholm on Moving Day, October 1st. "The camera goes into an apartment where some people are carrying things in and other people are taking everything out. The lady of the house has a very fussy husband, who opens every door. And the wife says, 'But I took everything. You don't need to worry.' He continues to open everything and in the kitchen finds some rice in a drawer. He yells to the wife, 'But you left the rice here.' The wife says, 'Oh, what is it? It is very little.' The man takes it out and it is exactly a handful, and he brings it over to the woman and says, 'But here is this.' She says, 'Oh, it's only a handful of rice. Throw it out.' And then came a voice on the screen which said, 'Only a handful of rice. But how was it gotten?' And the story follows, showing that a handful of rice could be a year's work.

"I began it with a wedding among the Maio people, where a boy and a girl get married. They have no land. So after the marriage the boy needs to go out and cut a clearing in the jungle and plow it up and start a rice field, or paddy. They are very poor and they have no animals; the man pulls the plow and the woman guides it. Finally they start to get a rice crop growing, and then comes a drought and there's no water for weeks, and the rice starts to die. So the boy leaves the wife and goes to the teakwood plantations in north Siam to tend elephants, and earns enough money to go home with. And when the harvest comes in, the entire crop is a handful of rice."

Two events stand out sharply among Paul's crowded activities

*This was released in 1940 as a Paul Fejos-Gunnar Skoglund Production, though Skoglund had really nothing to do with the shooting of the picture. Paul wrote at the time: "I do not worry about such things any more."

Paul and Axel Wenner-Gren in Southeast Asia, 1937

One of Paul's Komodo dragons on exhibit in Copenhagen, 1938

in these regions in 1937-38. He was shipwrecked on Komodo Island, near Sumbawa in the south East Indies, where he was lucky to escape alive. And he met Axel Wenner-Gren. The meeting with Wenner-Gren in Singapore was significant, for on this occasion he saved the life of the Swedish industrialist. Paul had a great gift for doing the right thing at the right moment.

The Komodo incident first. Paul thought it would be fun to photograph the giant Komodo dragon-lizards in their native habitat. Besides, the Swedish Crown Prince had asked him to get some specimens for the Royal Zoological Gardens in Stockholm.

There was no shipping to Komodo, but Paul, his radioman, and his cameraman took a Dutch ship which passed within ten miles of the island on its way to Australia. Its captain had agreed to transport and lower the high-speed launch which Paul had secured, and which would land them on Komodo, and then to return later and pick them up. Paul knew that because of great tide differentials there was a terrifically strong current in the narrow straits between Sumbawa and Komodo Island. Unfortunately a delay in launching his boat put the craft into the boiling waters at just the wrong time. Moreover, the Dutch maps of the area were notoriously inaccurate. The result was that the launch hit an unmarked coral reef, split up the middle, and then hung there on the coral rocks. The three men finally swam to shore safely, and succeeded in salvaging some rope and a flashlight or two.

Paul tells the story:

"I had real panic for the first time in my life when I found out that the eight running rivers which are marked on the map of Komodo were all dry-river beds. Obviously, the survey had been made during the rainy season, when there was running water. But at this time there wasn't a drop of water in there. And I found myself on this island, with my cameraman and my radio-man, and after two days of searching I couldn't find water anywhere. And then I panicked. I was alone when I panicked; I was up on a hill trying to find water somewhere. I was not looking for water on the hilltop, but I was there trying to look over the area, and it was uniformly brown and nowhere was it green.

"And then it struck home to me: How much longer can we survive on the island? I would say without water two- to two-and-a-half days; three days is about the maximum you can survive in tropical areas. And then I really panicked, panicked because I was unable to walk. I found out, on wanting to get back to my camp, that I couldn't walk at all, so I sat down. And then I tried to crawl, and I crawled all the way back to the camp. As soon as I was in the camp with the other people, this mental paralysis over my legs stopped, and I was able to walk again.

"Luckily, that night, we got saved, or rather, the next morning.

"About two o'clock in the morning my radioman came over to me and shook me to wake me up. I said, 'What is it?' He said, 'There is a ship along the horizon.' I said, 'You are crazy!' This was an area which was completely out of any shipping lanes, because the so-called Sape Strait runs between Sumbawa Island and the tiny flyspeck of Komodo Island. The current in this Strait is an exceedingly fast one. The island was known to have existed for a long, long time. Captain Bligh of the *Bounty* fame had sailed by it and wrote about this terrific current in his log book, but he never landed on the island. This is the reason the Komodo dragon was not known, because the approach to the island was so very difficult. There was simply no traffic; all the traffic was far north over to the Flores Sea and from there to Australia or to New Guinea. On the Timor Sea there was nothing. The only island is Christmas Island, which belongs to England and is far away. So I was positively sure that the boy was wrong.

"He said, 'No, I can really see the two lights, the mast lights.' I said, 'You didn't see any lights. That can't be anything else but a star.' Anyhow, I got up and walked over to a little hill with him and looked at it, and there were two lights there. But I still believed that they were stars. I took my compass and took a bearing and watched, and ten minutes later they had moved. So they were not stars; it was something moving.

"Luckily, we had some matches and we took some dry twigs and rapidly made a fire. We stupidly stood next to the fire and screamed our heads off, realizing that the sound would never reach as far as the ship, because the ship was so low on the horizon that all we could see were the lights on the mast and not the

61

navigational lights. We needed to get up to a higher place, and luckily the radioman had one flashlight which still had good batteries in it. He went up a tree and from the top of the tree started to flash an SOS toward the ship. After a good twenty minutes, suddenly I saw a light on board which sent back a message 'R.R.R.' received, received, received. Then I yelled up to the radioman and said, 'Tell them we are in trouble and need assistance.'

"Then came a message from the ship, again with lights, that they were unable to enter the Sape Strait now, but in the morning when the tides changed they would try to come and give us assistance.

"The next morning, I think about five o'clock, they lowered two lifeboats with coolies, and a young Dutch officer came over to the island. They took us off and also took our very damaged motor launch, which was in pieces practically, took it in tow and then hoisted it on the ship. We were off, and we went to Timor, the next scheduled stop for the ship. It was only later, when I returned to the island, that I found out it was partially inhabited. There was a tiny village on the opposite side of the island, behind large mountains, which contained about twelve or fourteen natives and which had been formerly a Dutch penal colony. It would have been inaccessible for help for us, however.

"A little later I went back to the blasted island, because I decided that I wouldn't allow it to lick me. But I went back with two native sailboats and many fresh coconuts. We drank coconut water during the whole time and were able to work. Also, I brought some extra coolies with me, and we trapped the dragons in traps which we constructed on the island. They were box, gravity-fall traps; a skeleton of a box was made with wood, and then chicken wire nailed on it all around. We put a dead goat inside, and about three days later when the goat smelled to high heaven, then the dragons came down, one after the other.

"The Komodo dragon was even then a protected animal; nobody was allowed to catch or shoot one. But when I told the Java officials what we had seen, they asked me please to try to catch one for the zoo in Java, if I went back. They gave me permission to capture or kill two animals for myself and to capture one for them, which I did. When I came back, they asked me how many were on the island, and I said, 'I haven't the slightest idea, but from what I saw and the frequency of the encounter, maybe three or four hundred, maybe more.'

"Of the two we captured and kept, one went to the Zoological Gardens in Stockholm, and one went to the Zoological Gardens in Copenhagen, where in due course they died, not from illness or climate, but from visitors. Some stupid visitor threw beer caps into the place and they ate them. One of them had a perforated intestine; we performed an autopsy on him later. The one which went to Stockholm was 14½ feet long, the Copenhagen one 13 feet."

A great deal of Paul Fejos emerges from this dramatic experience. The zest for adventure, and the way even his adventures fell into a pattern which would have needed little revising for a movie script; his honest confession of his fears; and above all, the determination to go back to the island. "I decided I wouldn't allow it to lick me." He had to maintain control.

His encounter with Axel Wenner-Gren was to have far-reaching results.

Wenner-Gren came to port in Singapore in his huge yacht, the *Southern Cross*, when Paul was not far inland on an expedition. Learning that he was near, Mrs. Marguerite Wenner-Gren sent him a note inviting him for dinner on board the yacht. It says something about the regal atmosphere in which the Wenner-Grens moved that she appended, there on the banks of the jungle, the notation: "Black tie." Paul was of course in bush clothing, and had to send back word to that effect. Whereupon another message was received: "Come as you are!" He and his wife Inga, who was with him at the time, went as they were.

Later Wenner-Gren wanted to go hunting and Paul arranged an expedition for him. They flushed a tiger and Paul, always the perfect host, stepped back to let the visitor have the kill. Wenner-Gren fired, but only wounded the animal. Then Paul noticed that Wenner-Gren's rifle was shaking violently, as was the man himself. He had bad buck fever. Paul moved in and shot the charging tiger about ten feet away, just as it was ready to leap.

63

So the agile Hungarian had saved the life of one of the richest men, presumably, in the world. From then on, for the next twenty years, Paul's life and that of Axel Wenner-Gren touched each other's frequently, in a relationship which became strangely frustrating at times, but which bent Paul's career into new and productive channels.

Chapter Four

ADVENTURE BY PLAN

———————————— ◆•◆ ————————————

FTER MAKING *A Handful of Rice* Paul returned to Scandinavia late in 1938 by way of the Indian Ocean and the Suez Canal. He was very ill on the trip with sprue, one of the more severely debilitating tropical diseases, endemic in many regions. It induces, among other things, a dangerous anemia. Fortunately Paul was medically sophisticated; he gave himself shots of liver extract throughout the voyage, and landed at Stockholm very weak but convalescent. He was now 42 years of age.

On December 31, 1939, he left for Peru with a fully equipped expedition sponsored by his new friend Wenner-Gren, who had extensive mineral interests in Peru. Paul knew that he was not a trained ethnographer; he was as much explorer here as scientist. The plan was to make contact with, study, and photograph a primitive tribe of Indians called the Mashco, at the headwaters of the Madre de Dios River in the upper Amazon Basin. First the expedition went inland to the Bolivian border, flying in all the equipment and personnel to the tiny frontier village of Maldonado in eastern Peru. From there it started up the river with four large canoes equipped with outboard motors, and one diesel-motor barge. They had a three-month food supply. The terrain was extremely difficult; it took the expedition weeks to negotiate an air distance of 90 miles, through rapids and around waterfalls, pulling the canoes out by block and tackle and cutting pathways through the forest to the next open space on the river. They pressed on south into the Rio Colorado, and on June 16th pitched their base camp three miles up-river. From there they began surveys by boat, and by a single-motor Condor hydroplane supplied by the Peruvian navy.

As Paul told the story later to a staff-writer from the New York *World-Telegram*, for two days they flew over palm-roofed huts of Mashco Indians, dropping packs of fishhooks, mirrors, whistles, and cloth as presents. The second day the plane motor misfired. The plane crashed into the river, the Rio Karene, 30 miles from camp, on a sandbank just opposite a Mashco village.

With his two Peruvian companions, Paul was at once surrounded by naked Mashcos armed with huge bows and arrows. He opened a sign-language conversation with the tribal chief, Payhaha. The Indians brought some bananas and birdskins as presents, but the three intruders decided that the course of discretion would be to live in the plane as a fortress until help might arrive.

The next morning they called the Indians again and tried to trade for a canoe. The only goods they had left were a watch, a handkerchief, and some naval epaulettes, none of which pleased the Indians. They demanded machetes, and became threatening. The three replied using significant sign language, with threats of invoking the ire of their huge duraluminum bird, and the Indians retreated. The explorers started trying to build a balsa raft, but night came before they finished, a tense night of whistling from bush to bush, mysterious calls. The adventure ended happily after four days, when a Peruvian army plane spotted the wreck and led a rescue motorboat party to the village.

Payhaha's clan, the Kareneri, later became friendly. But finally the whole ethnological venture was aborted by a tragically stupid series of human errors.

The Peruvian government had insisted that the party take with them the fourteen soldiers for their safety in an area of hostile Indians. Paul describes the subsequent events:

"Soon the trouble began. None of the accompanying Peruvian soldiers was bred in the montaña; they were all from Lima. Therefore, the montaña represented for them something fearful

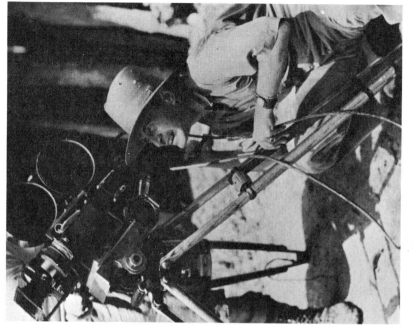

The doctor-ethnologist at work.

After forced landing of plane on Amazon expedition, 1940.

and they were constantly scared. If anywhere a twig broke, then they were immediately up, with hands on their rifles, and itchy fingers. Unfortunately, this led to a tragedy, because the geologist who was with me, Dr. Lowther, went up river on the Rio Colorado to get some geological specimens and was away from the camp for several days' distance. During this time, of course, the soldiers needed to go with him. I was happy about that, having the soldiers out of my camp, but was very worried about what would happen.

"Two days later at noon I had a radio schedule with them, and I found out from one of my men who went up with them, a transport officer, that they had reached the first Mashco camp, which I already knew of. And that they found the Indians very friendly, and the Indians were warning them not to go further up river, because the people are "bad" there, a hostile tribe. Well, this was no news for me. I had learned in New Guinea that almost everywhere primitive natives, if they have a fight with the neighboring tribe, always try to involve the white man in the fight because the white man has firearms and he's a good ally to have. And I warned them about this and told them that under no circumstances should they get together with these Indians, that they should give them some presents, and send them away from the camp.

"Then I closed up the transmitter. The next day at noon we had another transmission, and then the transport officer—he was a very young kid, about 19 or 20—told me, 'You must be wrong about these Indians. They are frightfully nice and they help us with the canoe,' and all this. And I said, 'What do you mean, help you with the canoe?' It developed that the Indians had offered to go with them, escort them up river, and they took the Indians along.

"So I bawled out the boy and said, 'Look, if those are such bad people, why do the Indians go with you? And watch out, you will get into a fight.' 'Oh, no, they are very nice.' Then that evening I had an extra schedule on the radio, just to be able to know what was happening, and I learned that during the afternoon when the Indians went ahead, suddenly they heard a terrific amount of noise, screaming and yelling, and all these

68

'friendly' Indians—the lower tribe—were running toward the camp. And the 'hostile' Indians from up river were running behind them, firing arrows. I knew this would be the case.

"I said to the boy, 'Well, what did you do?' He said, 'We fired.' 'What do you mean "fired"?' He said, well, he took his rifle and one other boy took his rifle and fired over their heads. I told him, 'It's awfully sad, because they were not after you, they were after the other Indians. Why in the heck did you fire? It is positively sure that you will have trouble within the next few hours.' 'Oh, no, they ran away the moment the first gun went off.'

"Unfortunately, I was a good prophet. The next day the whole outfit was lax up there, with no command. The carriers and also the soldiers decided to rest while Dr. Lowther was out hunting stones. The poor idiots walked out on a playa, a sandy beach, of the river, and left the canoes, and suddenly from the forest inside out came one arrow, which hit one of my carriers in the head. It did not wound him seriously; it had deflected over the bone and he had only a cut, nothing more.

"The corporal of the soldiers ran back to the canoes, where they had all their rifles, picked up a rifle and started firing. And in firing he hit one of the Indians, and then hit a second one, and then the Indians started to run into the forest. The corporal kept on firing and of course the firing was taken up by everyone who was there. How many of the Indians were hit, I have no idea; I was not there. I know that one was left dead on the beach.

"Well, this was horrible news for me, because it meant that I couldn't do any work. You can't do ethnography with a folk that is being killed and is trying to kill you. So I ordered them to turn around and come back with all speed, which they could do fairly easily down river. They returned without any further incident, but I had my first field trip where a life was lost. And I don't know, of course, how many of the Indians who went back into the bush had been hit.

"Then I reported this to the Governor of the area, who was very much surprised. 'Why do you report the death of an Indian? An Indian doesn't mean anything.' There were no other repercussions; nobody asked about it. When I came back I asked the authorities whether I needed to file a report on this or make out

an affidavit. 'Ah, not needed.' So there the chapter was closed.*
But for me it was a very sad première."

Paul returned to Cuzco and then to Lima, his expedition intact
but with no place to go. In the montaña he had come across Indians who told stories about buried cities in the mountains, inside
the jungle. He knew, of course, about Hiram Bingham's earlier
discovery of Machu Picchu, but he dismissed the Indian tales of
further cities as gossip. Then one day in the library of the Fran-
ciscan Monastery he found a book in Spanish called *The Brilliant
Future of Cuzco* (1848), which contained the story of a lay friar
who went from the monastery into the jungle, down to the
Oriente, to search for rare roots. He got lost and was away for
two years. When he returned he was sick, feverish, and he died a
few days later. But he spoke of some tremendous cities he had
seen in the jungle, with terrific columns.

This account placed these cities in exactly the same region in
which the Indians had reported them, and this in turn agreed
with a report Paul had from the Peruvian Inspector of Antiqui-
ties, via the American Embassy. The Inspector, Sr. Roberto
Rozas, had been led by two Indians (one of them Malpartido,
who had earlier reported finding such a city accidentally) to
the site of Phuyu Pata Marka, overgrown by vegetation. The
rumors were true! This was enough for Paul to get from Wenner-
Gren authorization to proceed with a new expedition, and he left
Cuzco in September 1940. He hoped not merely to examine and
uncover Phuyu Pata Marka but to discover and clear other sites
as well.

He was joined on the first leg of his expedition by another
Paul, Paul Hanna, a professor of Education at Stanford University, under conditions more than a little strange. Hanna had
been sent down to South America by Nelson Rockefeller, then
Coordinator of Latin American Affairs, to examine the extent
of German penetration, particularly in education, into the life
of Peru, Ecuador, and Bolivia. He discovered that there had been
a great deal of such penetration. German textbooks teaching the

*But Paul did file a very detailed report with the Peruvian authorities. The
incident had upset him greatly.

philosophy of National Socialism were in common use since Hitler had come into power. And the National Socialists had set up in every city an elementary-through-secondary school system where the students were taught Nazi doctrines.

About this time Paul Fejos arrived from the Madre de Dios with his half-dozen technicians and began asking questions about mounting another expedition. Was this a new kind of Nazi penetration? After all, it *was* an Axel Wenner-Gren-sponsored outfit. So Hanna, under instruction from the American Embassy in Lima, was sent along to see what he could find out. He joined the expedition at Cuzco as someone who knew about archeology, and since Paul Fejos was hungry for an archeologist he took Hanna along with him. By the time he discovered that he did not have an authenticated archeologist on his hands, Paul Hanna, for his part, had found out that Fejos loathed Hitler and all his works—that he was glad, indeed, to be in South America so that he could not, by his accident of nationality, be drawn into the European imbroglio on the side of Hungary. The little adventure into espionage was over. The two men became good friends. Hanna returned to Lima at this point.

During the short time that Paul Hanna was with the expedition he had the exciting experience of going out from Machu Picchu with a scouting party (which included Malpartido) which found the old narrow paved highway which ran along the narrow mountain ridge from Machu Picchu to Phuyu Pata Marka. With Paul Fejos and others he traversed the difficult road, sometimes crawling on his belly around narrow corners where the drop was sheer to the valley thousands of feet below, and reached the buried city.

In 1911 Hiram Bingham, later to become Governor of Connecticut and U.S. Senator, had begun a systematic exploration in southern Peru and had located the site of Machu Picchu, the largest of the ancient Inca cities. In 1912 he returned and cleared Machu Picchu from the forest and vegetation. Two later expeditions, in 1914 and 1915, mapped a good deal of the neighboring region, excavated the site of Llacta Pata, and discovered part of a network of roads connecting the cities which had formed the old pre-Columbian civilization. Bingham noted the sites of some of these cities but left most of them untouched. His expedition had gone along the old Inca road, had visited Phuyu Pata Marka and described it briefly in its buried condition, but had done no more with it.

The Wenner-Gren expedition did not concern itself with the Bingham excavations, which by 1940 (with the exception of Machu Picchu itself, which had been cleared again after many years and made accessible by Peruvian archeologists), had been reclaimed by tangled overgrowth. Paul sought out additional Inca ruins in a new area. During its two visits (September to December 1940, and July to November 1941) the expedition made topographic surveys, mapping in detail some 36 square kilometers in the Cordillera Vilcabamba—a chain of magnificent mountains—between the Urubamba River and its tributary the Aobamba, upstream from Machu Picchu. Five of the largest ruins were cleared of their thick vegetation, mapped, and photographed. Five smaller cities were examined and information obtained about the complex systems of roads, terraces, and lookout platforms between the sites. Since there were no archeologists with the expedition there was no attempt at scientific excavation.

This simple statement of accomplishment gives no hint of the massive difficulties encountered by any such expedition in the contiguous mountain-jungle area of the Andes. At a site named Choquesuysuy, which was at the bottom of the canyon of the Urubamba, the noon temperature in October was 98 degrees Fahrenheit, whereas at Phuyu Pata Marka, a site which was cleared at the top of a ridge 12,000 feet high, the noon temperature was 45 degrees and fell well below freezing at night.

The first exploration was terminated in December 1940, partly because of the rigors of the climate and partly because, as Paul wrote later, "It was impossible to organize a larger personnel and to obtain the necessary implements for large-scale deforestation of the area." These difficulties were overcome the following year, and the work of clearing the sites proceeded. The Peruvian government had made it possible for the expedition to secure the services, at various times, of 200 to 900 laborers.

Paul thrived on what was new and different. An expedition such as this engaged a whole range of his abilities. He was map-

Paul at Choquesuysuy on the Andes expedition, 1941.

maker, radio technician (if the radio conked out), physician at times of accident or illness, director of photography, organizer of work crews, arbiter of human relations, manager of logistics, publicity representative when newspapers and magazines began to seek him out—master, really, of the immense articulation of effort needed if an expedition is not to flounder.

Paul Hanna remembers the massive amounts of equipment with which Paul Fejos travelled on an expedition. Trunks and trunks of all kinds of survey instruments, medicines, books, geological equipment, gasoline lanterns, and even electric generators for radio transmission and for electric lights. For transport, he had leased the railway running from Cuzco up to Urubamba, the taking-off place for the tortuous trip by foot and mule-back to Machu Picchu. But all these supplies—to say nothing of much of the food necessary to support such a large expedition during its stay above the clouds—had eventually to be broken down into smaller bundles so that it could be back-packed by the Indian porters.

It was all organized with scientific care, and at the same time was very human. Even here Paul was always the artist; he sensed the human dimensions of the past while he was directing its uncovering. Once, high up in the Andes, above almost all vegetation, he arrived at an ancient stairway swept clean by the wind, unseen by human eye and untouched by human foot for no one knew how many hundreds of years. "When I stepped on the stairway," he said later, "I got horribly scared. A cold shiver ran up and down my back and I looked all around to see if an Inca official was coming from somewhere. It was so new and so real, and so unused, and so unlike an isolated ruin that I almost expected that at any minute someone would put his hand on my shoulder and say 'What are you doing here?' "

Axel Wenner-Gren visited one of the sites while the expedition was still working on it. He asked if he couldn't do something, and Paul, to keep the financier busy, set him drilling holes for dynamite in the rock where a road had to be blasted. Axel enjoyed it—and got a note of commendation in the published account of the expedition. The book, written by Paul, was the third in the *Viking Fund Publications in Anthropology*, newly insti-

74

tuted when The Viking Fund came into existence and continuing today as a series under the same general title. It was called *Archeological Explorations in the Cordillera Vilcabamba, Southeastern Peru* (1944).

The first book in the same series, also by Paul, was *Ethnography of the Yagua* (1943), the report of an interim Peruvian expedition made when weather and lack of supply interrupted the first phase of the Inca researches. Here he was in Peru, facing the prospect of six idle months before he could resume the hunt for buried cities. Why not explore something else? Perhaps make an ethnological film study of a little-known Indian tribe? He still had on hand the geologist, G. Kenneth Lowther; a cameraman, Norman Matthews; an electrical sound expert, H. R. Besserman; and Albert Giesecke, Jr., to place in charge of the difficult problem of supply. Thus was mounted the expedition to the Yagua tribe in northeastern Peru between the Putumayo and Amazon rivers, along the shallow tributaries of the Amazon. This between December 1940, and July 1941.

Paul selected the Yagua for investigation because it was among the least known of the lowland Peruvian tribes and had been the object of no systematic study. Its members had resisted all attempts to civilize them, including, over the years, those of missionaries. They had not been hostile to the missionaries, for they were a peaceful people. They simply preferred the splendid isolation of their own culture, and wanted to be left alone. The expedition visited twelve of the 25 to 35 clans composing the total tribe of some 1,000 people. The Amazon basin in which they lived, the montaña, is a vast tropical forest plain, at all places less than a thousand feet above sea-level. Rivers proved to be the only means of travel through the dense trackless jungle. The average temperature was 78 degrees and the relative humidity about ninety-nine.

So Paul and the other members of his party lived with this primitive folk—essentially a hunting tribe—gained their confidence, learned their language and studied their ways of life, their social institutions, their arts and amusements, their religion and mythology, to say nothing of their hunting techniques with their blow-gun weaponry. They were a good-looking people with

75

tawny skins, their hair lighter than that of most Indians. As a token of their trust and acceptance Paul was given a Yagua name and allowed to sleep in the community house of the Ant Clan, a privilege seldom accorded to strangers.

Here the ethnologist-motion-picture-director came into his own once more. He had brought along a camera equipped with sound-recording devices, with which he had hoped to make a faithful record of the Yagua language and some of the tribe's social customs. It developed, in fact, into much more of a production than that. He was able to get the Yaguas to reproduce one of the clan migrations down-river to a new living-site, an event that occurred only rarely, once a generation, perhaps, when the floor of their large main house was filled with the bones of their dead, or when game became scarce in their hunting-terrain, events which usually seemed to coincide.

He shot thousands of feet of film, and edited it later as a record of migration. The Yagua proved to be excellent natural actors, as eager to dramatize their lives for the camera as any Hollywood starlet. The shaman, or medicine-man, acted as "director," and realized by himself, Paul said, the necessity of rehearsing "scenes" and assigning "roles" in advance to avoid confusion. The director of *Broadway* discovered that he had little to do except to see that the "actors" appeared when there was plenty of sunshine and stood within range of the camera. "The Yagua . . . found it vastly amusing to reenact their cultural tradition and customs."* So said Paul. One is aware, however, that his shrewd selection of what was to be photographed must have controlled a good deal of the production. Paul had invented a new field technique: that of getting natives to re-enact for the camera significant aspects of their culture. The film was, and is, an extraordinary ethnographical achievement.

After the Yagua, back to the high Andes and its vanished civilizations for the second time. And then, in December 1941, the return to the relative civilization of New York City. Paul landed on December 7th, Pearl Harbor Day.

Ethnography of the Yagua, p. 29.

Paul directing the film of the Yagua migration, 1941

77

By this time the Viking Fund had been established as a corporate reality, with offices in Rockefeller Center.

Paul was by now deeply committed to ethnology and indeed to all aspects of anthropology. Based on the experience gained from field trips he had had dreams of getting Wenner-Gren to underwrite further anthropological research. Axel could easily have released a small part of his huge holdings in support of such a cause. He was not averse to liquidating an enterprise in order to invest the capital in another which seemed potentially more lucrative, but he did not give money away easily where it was not likely to work for him. The establishment of the Viking Fund in 1941 came about as the result of a series of happy accidents— happy, that is, from the point of view of generations of anthropologists who have profited from Wenner-Gren's gift.

In 1941 Wenner-Gren had not yet been put on the blacklist, though the IRS, which had been watching his financial activities for some time, had begun a multi-million-dollar suit against him. Wenner-Gren decided to use the proceeds of the business transaction which the government was challenging to found the Viking Fund, which he endowed with two-and-a-half million dollar's-worth of shares in the Electrolux Company and the Servel Corporation. "Science" was served by Wenner-Gren's generosity, and anthropology was to have a new benefactor.

It took some explaining a little later to make Axel understand that a U.S. foundation, established in February 1941 under the laws of the State of Delaware, was not a holding company the funds of which could serve the business interests of its founder. In fact the Viking Fund, both morally and legally, had to be more circumspect than any wife of Caesar's, and its performance through the years has been exactly that. In 1951, all turmoils forgiven and forgotten, the name was changed to The Wenner-Gren Foundation for Anthropological Research. Wenner-Gren himself had of course never been a member of the Board of the Foundation, and had never influenced its activities.

Before the United States was very far into World War II Axel Wenner-Gren had been put on the blacklist of the State Department—a circumstance which needs a little historical clarification.

It is often assumed that there is tar on the fingers of any international manipulator of large enterprises, but in retrospect the charges against Wenner-Gren as a Nazi collaborator were even more naïve than the man himself. Wenner-Gren was essentially a man of peace, and when the prospect of war loomed in Europe he said that he used his his connections to interview Göring, with the quaint notion that he might persuade Göring to persuade Hitler to stop his sabre-rattling. Rumor distorted this quixotic sortie into a suspicious relationship between the Swedish industrialist and the Nazi hierarchy.

One other incredible episode added fuel to a fire that was almost self-starting. On September 3, 1939, Wenner-Gren was beginning a voyage across the Atlantic in the *Southern Cross* when his captain received a radio SOS, just west of the Hebrides, that the British merchant ship *Athenia* had been torpedoed and was sinking—the first such incident of the war. The captain urged Wenner-Gren to turn about and retreat to safety as fast as possible. "No," said Axel, "if people are drowning we must try to help them." So they steamed toward the scene of the disaster and picked up several hundred survivors. They brought them into port wrapped, some of them, in Mrs. Wenner-Gren's furs or in Oriental rugs from the ship's cabins.

Shortly afterward the rumor-factory started. "Wasn't it strange that the yacht of Wenner-Gren, the Nazi confidant, was so near the *Athenia* when it was torpedoed by the Germans? Didn't this smell of plot?" Just what might have been gained by such a plot was beyond anyone's comprehension, but the rumors spread and grew. Before long the innocent Swede, really twice the victim of his humanitarianism, was put on the blacklist, and removed from it only several years later when the charges against him were formally recognized as unfounded.

But the Viking Fund was born and lived for a time under a dark star. Not much wonder that Paul Fejos, in the beginning, had trouble giving money away.

Paul's relation with Axel Wenner-Gren was always close but ambivalent. Wenner-Gren liked and trusted him, but that very trust created for Paul some difficult quanderies over the years. He owed a great deal to the Swede, who by his subsidization of various expeditions and most notably by endowing the Viking Fund had made possible Paul's last and perhaps his most productive career. Paul never forgot this, and part of his attitude toward Axel was that of the grateful subject to the Grand Seigneur—a sort of Renaissance recognition of station and patronage. Officially he was always the Great Founder, the Great Philanthropist. At the same time Paul was often disturbed and sometimes made furious by the financier's ruthless business code and by his consuming devotion not so much to money itself as to the power that lives with money—a common pattern. Thus Paul lived in a kind of love-hate relationship with the man who used him time and again, but whom Paul bent toward benevolent purposes which Wenner-Gren would never otherwise have dreamed of. Like many men of power, he was seduced into philanthropy.

Axel was a simple man in many ways, affectionate, gentle, amiable, and as we have seen, in a curious way naïve. He took understandable pride in being self-made, and as his formidable empire grew around the world it included everything from vacuum cleaners to Swedish guns and timber to Mexican silver, railways, and telephone companies, to South American ore and vast Canadian land and mining holdings. Part of Paul's influence, informally, was occasionally to protect the man against himself. He wanted Wenner-Gren, as a man and friend, to live up to what he, Paul, saw as the high demands of his position. Wenner-Gren trusted Paul because he knew that he was in the deepest personal sense faithful to him.

Part of Wenner-Gren's essential simplicity was shown in the way he received the tributes and honors with which men of power become familiar—not with any display of arrogance, but simply as if they came in the normal way of life.

He knew nothing of anthropology, though he endowed it and always praised it, commending it (in speeches that Paul wrote for him) as a proper object of support for "humanity." Such was the clean directness of his unostentatious self-possession that it took him into some adventures that were breath-taking—not for him, but for those sponsoring his appearances. Once at a major eastern university he delivered, before an audience of selected anthropological scholars, an address that Paul had composed for him. He got through it successfully, and finally must have convinced himself that he had written it. At its conclusion he laid down the manuscript and asked, as one scholar to others: "Any questions?" The situation was saved by Paul's leaping into the breach and getting someone to deflect the discussion.

Paul loved Wenner-Gren, and was unhappy that he loved him. But he wept when he died. Wenner-Gren was a man easy to censure but difficult to dislike, face to face. At least some of the good he did lived after him. It seemed strange that in his latter years he fell into the hands of bad financial advisors (this was another part of his naïveté) but by his death in 1961 his own empire had pretty well diminished.

The Viking Fund had been established with such celerity that its exact functions were initially ambiguous, beyond the usual "philanthropic, charitable, educational, etc." declarations common to such foundations. Before long Paul had convinced Wenner-Gren that in the interests of knowledge the Fund should devote itself exclusively to the support of anthropological research. There was no such foundation existing in the country.

In the truest if not the most obvious sense Paul was preordained to his new career of directing the Fund. He lacked the exact academic credentials common to those heading such enterprises in the United States, but he had a far deeper and more imaginative understanding of what he wanted to do—indeed, of what needed to be done—than most dispensers of philanthropic funds.

Chapter Five

PROFESSOR FEJOS

———————◆ • ◗—————————

THE VIKING FUND WAS STILL an infant when the Second World War closed in. Anthropologists who had studied remote peoples in the Pacific and knew something about landing beaches or native customs found themselves suddenly "informants" for government. A good many universities had become, in part, training schools for young men who needed specialized instruction. Stanford University was one of these; in 1942 it established several units within the Army Specialized Training Program. One of these was a Far Eastern Area and Language Program which gave a six-month's intensive training in languages—Malay, Chinese, Dutch, and Japanese—plus as much knowledge of the geography, history, and cultures of the Pacific and Far East as could be crowded in. Staff members who taught in the program still remember it as one of the most satisfying academic experiences in their careers. Working under the pressure of a national emergency, historians, sociologists, political scientists, geographers, anthropologists and language teachers submerged their disciplinary differences and their individual whimsies to achieve a coordinated common program. No one talked much about "inter-disciplinary studies," themselves still very new then on the academic horizon. The people simply did the job. From the students' point of view, they were receiving instruction which might save their lives six months later on some distant atoll or hostile shore. And although the academic atmosphere was not exactly one of fine careless rapture, it was extraordinarily intense and, within its military limits, broadly educational.

Because of the war-time dislocations of ordinary academic and foundation activities, the demands of the Viking Fund on Paul's time could easily be adjusted to part-time public service. He went to Stanford for two six-month periods in 1943-44, and for a later training period for Navy personnel who might serve as military administrators.

Paul was a one-man interdisciplinary university. He knew both the theory and practice of "how to get along with natives" when you land on a lonely beach, and he became one of the most exciting if unorthodox teachers ever seen at Stanford. The students loved him. Before anyone had ever heard of "role-playing" as a teaching device, he created classroom situations which posed problems for the trainees demanding excellence and imagination for their solution. In a sense, Paul was a motion-picture director in everything he ever did, and here were dramatic devices and pedagogy and personal magnetism and enthusiasm and solid know-how all orchestrated in a controlled production aimed at precise results. Paul thought of his informal classroom manner, his careful lack of academic decorum, his "baseball English," as perhaps unsettling to the academic image. As a matter of fact his colleagues admired his wide knowledge and his ability to translate it into vivid terms. They admired him so much they never thought of envying him.

He was living his new life with great gusto. He had re-married after his return from Peru,* this time to Marianne Arden, whom he had met on shipboard on his way back from Europe to New York, prior to his departure for Peru. The charming Marianne, who had made something of a career as a *chanteuse*, used to play the piano and sing for the boys on many occasions. Paul and his bride lived in a little house on the Stanford campus, where he would sit up late into the night structuring problems for the next day's classes. He loved the whole assignment, and he communicated in his own words the pleasure he took in teaching what he always called "How to make friends and influence people in primitive societies." As he said:

*He and Inga Arvad were divorced on June 3, 1942.

"I had a whale of a time. All these boys were from all sorts of varied life, varied vocations in life; and also they were from varied areas of the United States. And I liked to explain to a Southern boy that though a man may be coal black, he is his equal. And to some extent I succeeded.

"I departed from the regular lecture courses, and brought in something which I thought would be more functional. It was a three-ring circus, but it worked. I first would draw on the blackboard a map of a mythical island in the Pacific, and then ask for volunteers from the class. I told them that they were a task force—sometimes of 30, sometimes of 10, sometimes 6 people— with a certain objective; for instance, they might need to erect a radio direction-finding station on an island. And I then told them to proceed. 'I am your eyes, ears, and nose. Whatever you want to know about what you see, hear or smell, ask it, and I'll tell you what it is.' And then the native language-teachers we had, plus some other instructors, were given roles. The boys from the class were told, 'All right. You've arrived at such-and-such point on the island. There is the map. This is where you are. What do you do now? You're unpacked, the Navy dropped you, the Navy is away, tell me what do you do next.'

"They were never confronted with any combat problem. We took it for granted that the island would be free of Japanese and Japanese stragglers. They were to proceed, for example, to put up the direction-finder. From the very first they found out that they could not do it without native help. So they needed to locate a native village somewhere, and then I made it quite tough for them to find out who the natives on the island were, what kind, of what culture. And then they would proceed to make friends with the people.

"I took care that in the evolution of this thing any mistake they made rebounded 50 times. And then they needed to find out what was wrong. So, for instance, if a boy was very imperious and ordered instead of asking, I made sure that he would have later difficulty; the native became uncommunicative or didn't tell something which was important. This turned out to be a damn useful way of teaching and also made them realize that to learn Malay or to learn Chinese was exceedingly important, because

84

without it they wouldn't be able to communicate. They had received a number of communication tricks: that is, what to do when you don't know the language, but of course this was not sufficient. Soon I saw that on the chow line they were talking to each other in Chinese or in Malay, because they started to realize that now they were not learning for a degree or for an examination, but really to save their own necks, and that really worked wonders.

"As far as staff was concerned, I could have had any instructor or any professor from Stanford University. Felix Keesing was there, an anthropologist for the Program, so he helped me a lot. And I had great help from a Professor of German, A. E. Sokol, who was an Austrian and had been educated in Vienna, and when World War I ended there, had found himself without anything to do because originally he was in the Austro-Hungarian Navy, a frigate lieutenant. So he signed a contract with a Dutch steamship company and went out as second mate on a Dutch boat all over the Indies and cruised there for something like three years. During this time he learned, of course, fluent Malay, and got quite a lot of knowledge about the islands and some of the cultures. He was a real help, particularly in these reenactments of things we were doing.

"These boys got good training. I devised an examination for them which did not include writing any papers or answering any questions, but they were simply told, 'You are now on a plane the destination of which you do not know. You are going out somewhere into the Pacific. It's night. During the night suddenly the sergeant in the plane shakes you and tells you you must bail out. You bail out of the plane, and you hit land. I am your eyes, ears and nose; tell me, where did you land and how will you proceed to get back to the Army?'

"So they landed, and they asked me, 'On what did I land?' I said, 'Sand.' Then a boy would ask: 'What do I see? What do I see in front of me? What do I see northward?' So I said, 'Northward you are seeing the sea only.' Then he asked, 'What do I see southward?' 'Southward you see gardens, native gardens.' Then he asked, 'What form are they?' And as they had knowledge already of how these settlements looked, and as the garden forms and agricultural patterns are distinctive in each culture, he was able to deduce where he was. And then they had quite a lot of information about what the integrating factor of the culture was. They learned which area was given over to hunting, which was agriculture, which was this, which was that; so they started to search. Before they met the first native on the island, they already had a vague idea about where they were located.

"When they met a native, I usually played that part. And then came the point of making friends. Or they did not meet natives at all, but arrived at a village and found it deserted, and deserted recently, with fireplaces still warm. What would they do? Then came the need of going after the natives and trying to induce them to return, and making friends with them. They really did marvelously."

Unless one appraises them in terms of liberal education, the carefully-constructed area and language programs at Stanford were largely wasted. Most of the men, originally pointed at some sort of service in military government, were finally assigned to the Signal Corps, but instead of making friends on islands in the Far East or South Pacific, many of them spent the rest of the war learning how to string telephone lines in Missouri, where they "learned to make friends," perhaps, with Missouri farmers' daughters. Some went to the European theater, a few to India. Though we did win the war, such dislocations were not unknown in army life. For the trainees it was perhaps a little safer, if not quite as exciting.

Paul was always warmly remembered at Stanford, and he served (mostly *in absentia*) as Consulting Professor of Anthropology until his death. He had other academic appointments, at Columbia, Fordham, and also notably at Yale, where he was Lecturer in Anthropology, with professorial rank. He used to travel to New Haven to give seminars in which, among other things, he would try to instruct graduate students in the importance of photography as a tool in studying native peoples. Frequently he was more frustrated than encouraged as he saw that these embryo researchers not only did not know what to photograph but could not *read* a photograph with anthropological correctness. Over the years Paul tried to bring his experience as a maker of ethnological motion pictures to the service of the profession. Occasionally he felt he was making progress; much of the time he was discouraged, for correct film-making involves *seeing* what to shoot as well as shooting it, and as a film expert he knew how the truth of a scene can be distorted by poor camera work or poor editing.

He was in fact a perfectionist, annoyed by people who worked at less than their full potential and impatient with his own successes because they were never quite what his sense of the ideal told him they should have been. If he cooked a dinner (which he did superbly) it was never, in all respects, good enough for his guests. When he uncovered a dozen Inca cities he was depressed because he had no archeologists along with him, and he himself was not archeologist enough to do the proper scientific excavating.

His modesty must have seemed assumed to some people, in the face of the obvious excellence of his performance. It was very real, however, edging at times into an honest feeling of inferiority; he seldom measured his own abilities fairly. He knew he was a good movie director, a sound ethnologist; he *had* to, for the recognition he received was unequivocal. But when people told him he was good he was afraid they didn't really think so. He had a vision of the way things ought to be, artistically, esthetically, ethically. He did various things to prove to himself that he could do them (this was part of his restlessness) and then felt he had to do something else where he might succeed more fully. What he had done didn't satisfy his standard of what his performance *should* have been.

Perhaps this was because Paul was always the *artist* in his multiple careers. His first-class mind, his ceaseless ingenuity, his daring, intellectual and physical, his acute intuitions of people and places and things—all these were creatures of this drive toward perfection which left him a little unhappy about a good many people and often unhappy with himself. But he had more tolerance for others than for himself; ahead of him was always the impossible dream.

Frederic Fellini has been quoted as saying:* "An artist who realizes a dream always senses a diminishment. . . . An image in the unconscious is not framed; it has the fascination of the vague and indefinite, of the inexpressible. This obscurity makes it more exciting. But when you realize the idea, you have taken away the mystery, the imprecision that makes things more than just themselves. The authentic, happy artist is one who maintains some sense of the arcane."

Much of this could be said of Paul. In this last sense he *was* the happy artist; the sense of the arcane was very close to him. Reared as a Catholic he was without formal religion and had little use for dogma (though he did ask for last rites when he knew he was dying). He believed, rather, that a person is one with nature, that in life and death he is a part of the life-process. The love-mercy principle of religion was also congenial to him.

Like many others, he had some deep-seated superstitions. If you left a coat in a restaurant you never went back for it— bad luck. If a swallow killed itself on the windshield of his car he would be emotionally upset the rest of the day. This sense of the mysterious would emerge when he discussed the magic of primitive peoples. He liked to point out that Western society is as susceptible to magic and superstition, in a different frame of reference, as any primitive society. As he put it:

"We don't call it magic; we give some other name to it. If any anthropologist should come to us from New Guinea, a Papuan, and do an ethnological survey of the U.S., magic would loom very large in it, from knocking on wood to not walking under a ladder, or even to the acceptance of science, for much of that with us is magic. If I have a patient and I want to run a series of chest X-rays on him, he doesn't know what's happening; he couldn't read the X-ray, he doesn't know how the X-ray works. He will accept this alone on the magical value of my standing as a physician; he knows it. Just take a look at advertising on television, for instance, in the U.S. Ninety percent is magic, except the magic is in the form of a scientific-sounding name. So they will say that you must use a toothpaste of such-and-such kind because it contains "irium." Now you go and pull out your

*In an interview by Charles Thomas Samueles, *The Atlantic,* April 1972, p. 86.

chemistry books, and you find that there is no element called irium. Then you go to a chemical dictionary and you can't find it. This is a name which some advertising man invented on upper Park Avenue; it sounded good. But for the audience it is real, it is magic. People accept this because it has a strange name that *sounds* authentic, though in reality it's totally meaningless."

In an address to the New York Academy of Medicine,* Paul pointed out again that magic is not the monopoly of savages.

"On Soembawa Island, lives a shaman in the village of Do Dongo. Across his chest is tattooed a large circle with an ornamental capital letter B. He is my good friend and colleague, the shaman of the Dongo tribe. The story of his tattoo is a case in point. He was my principal informant in 1937 when I was doing field work on the ethnology of his tribe. We became fast friends through the several months of close association. He taught me native medicine and I occasionally helped out with his cases when he asked for my assistance or wanted me in consultation. All my drugs in the medicine chests originated from the German Bayer Company, and on the packing cases was painted their trademark, an ornamented B in a circle. As I had taken all my 'magical' supplies from such cases, my friend came to associate the power of my magic with the design of the trademark. After several months, he very formally asked my permission to use my magical symbol. Shamans are usually governed by very strict ethics. Less ethically, and without the permission of the Bayer Company, I released the copyright, and the letter B within the circle was emblazoned on my friend's chest. It gave him a tremendous additional amount of 'mana,' and *de facto* increased his curative powers.

"I am not being facetious about this, and I ask you to realize that for the primitive concept of medicine these things are just as real and valid as our most cherished theories in serology or in the chemistry of the endocrine glands. . . .

"We Westerners have our magical practices as well, though we label them as traditions or superstitions. When next you receive a prescription from your scientifically trained physician,

*Man's Image in Medicine and Anthropology, International Universities Press, 1963, pp. 55-56.

remember that the RX on the top left corner is really an invocation to a deity* for effective work of that prescription. I trust you will remember also that your physician's theories and knowledge are *not* based on magical theories, but on scientific facts. Nevertheless—though disappearing at a very rapid rate and with great acceleration—magic is still present in our time in our modern medicine. This is not 'bad.' It is an important adjunct to our chemotherapy, our surgery, our science, and above all to the art of medical practice. It is not trickery; it is not malicious intent to deceive."

He might have added that the placebo, which is little less than magic as any primitive would understand it, has an honored place in present-day medical practice.

*Robert Hooper wrote in his *Lexicon Medicum*, N.Y., 1836: ". . . the character which we today place at the head of our prescriptions, and which is understood and is supposed to mean *recipe*, is a relict of the astrological symbol of Jupiter. . . ."

Chapter Six

THE FOUNDATION:
ADVENTURES OF THE MIND

———◆•◆———

T HE VIKING FUND HAD AN unostentatious beginning. Its administrative structure was very simple; Paul, with the title at first of Director of Research (he became President later) was always the effective managing officer. He had a small Board of three or four businessmen, headed by Richard C. Hunt, a distinguished New York lawyer—and a fine man—who knew Paul's abilities and gave him a free hand in running the foundation. In fact, one of Paul's concerns was that he should always be checked closely; the Board would meet to review whatever programs or expenditures he presented. It was all pretty informal and in its early days unformed. Here was the only foundation ever created to meet the needs of the anthropological profession. What were those needs?

Whatever they were, most of them had to be served at first by small grants, for the Viking Fund (and indeed the Wenner-Gren Foundation as it became) was by no means one of the large foundations in terms of available income.* Hence the importance of flexibility, the possibility of making *some* substantial grants but more frequently quick grants to help a scholar over a hump, or to be used as money to help get a project started which might later flower on its own. The interests of the founda-

---

*The capitalization grew over the years, without the infiltration of any new funds, from a little less than two-and-one-half million dollars in 1941 to some twenty-four million in 1972. It had reached over twelve million before Paul died in 1963.

91

tion were limited to anthropology, but even within that field there were many sub-branches competing for funds: archeology, physical anthropology, cultural anthropology, linguistics. Since the emphasis could not be placed on large "projects" it was placed on *people*—their research, fellowships, travel, publications. Above all, the influence of the foundation on the discipline of anthropology stemmed in great part from Paul's canny awareness of what was alive in anthropology and even more from his gut feelings of what ought to be made to come alive.

There is a seeming paradox here. As time went on, the most respected senior anthropologists kept saying that Paul, in his brief career in the field, had brought a gain of a hundred years to anthropology, that he had helped shift the center of gravity of a whole academic discipline. Paul himself once told an interviewer that in earlier days by the expenditure of $200,000 in the right place at the right time the whole direction of development in the field of anthropology could be changed. There is probably a little Hungarian exaggeration there, but the point is that he went ahead immediately to insist that he had never tried to make this change, that trying to play God was furthest from his thoughts. The image he presented to the profession, and the one that he saw of himself, was that of a man simply trying to do what scholars wanted him to do. He did admit that he liked "risk" projects, the subsidization of ventures that no other foundation would touch. The difference came in Paul's understanding of which people and projects could open new windows for anthropology. One can accept his honest self-analysis of never having tried consciously to tell anthropology where it should go. The facts of his career, however, depending, to be sure, upon his *selection of people*, not on his instructing them, disprove his modest disclaimers. He was capable of grasping imaginatively a problem that needed a solution and then going out to find the men who might consciously solve it. If you believe, for example, as Paul did, that ignorance of and indeed contempt for sophisticated instrumentation was a defect of those engaging in field work, whether archeological or ethnographic, you would begin to look for anthropologists who felt as you did—and you might even make them grants!

Paul in early 1940s after the establishment of The Viking Fund

Paul in 1952 at the "Anthropology Today" conference

It was the nature of his office that he had to discourage many requests for funds. When a grant was made, however, he had the ability to make the recipient feel that he was somehow doing the Foundation and Paul himself a favor in accepting the money. Any visitor who went out of his office knew that Paul's attention while he had been there was entirely his. Paul could praise people, though he was not given to flattery, but above all, he *listened*—and there are few people, anthropologists or not, whose sense of well-being is not enhanced by being encouraged to talk.

In spite of his love of science, a lot of Paul's education of others began with his curious non-American attitude toward the "science" of anthropology. Some American social scientists had been spending a good deal of time aping the methods of science in order to show that their socially-oriented studies were truly "scientific" and objective. This had led, frequently, to purely descriptive and repetitive reporting, shunning all questions of "values" (unless they could be tabulated and measured) as being unscientific. Paul had a strange lack of respect for the ordinary abracadabra of the social sciences, of which anthropology was one. He innocently held that anthropology should be one of the humanities (being unaware, at first, of strict American academic demarcations). He was interested in the study of man in all his varieties and all his complexities and confusions, and he saw anthropology as a possible means to this (humanistic) end. For by anybody's standard he was a humanist. Central to his code, and strengthened by his multiple contacts with primitive peoples, was his deep belief that "all human beings have dignity, and this is terribly important to them."

Moreover, he was capable of arguing, even bullying, his colleagues in anthropology into accepting new methods and techniques of research, and into refining old methods. We shall see some examples of this; no man who claimed so little ever did so much.

Take internationalism, for example. Paul found too many anthropologists in the United States, even after the war, academically provincial and insular, largely uninterested in what was being done by anthropologists in other lands. They had explored kinship relations in every conceivable primitive society, to be sure, and then had trained their students to go back to the same societies (there were only so many of them available) and explore the same kinship relations all over again. Frequently, because the field work was easier in the United States, it was done with the American Indian.

As Paul put it: "The North American Indian, number one, is not primitive; number two, he does not have a free society but is living in a laboratory situation. The results the students bring back are catastrophic. They don't realize when they go out that the Navajos, for instance, may know more about anthropology than they do. Frequently they say something to a student and the student writes it down, and then they say, 'No, don't write it. The anthropologist who was here last summer has it already.' " He felt, in his more discouraged moments, that "man is now getting out of anthropolgy. It is the Science of Man, but man is getting out of it."

He went on (referring to anthropology as it was in the fifties):

"We have today immensely learned young gentlemen who know everything about, let's say, funeral customs on the Trobriand Islands, or others who know everything about the economy of the Nicobars, but at the same time they will not know that there is a world around them. Man is falling out; potsherds are becoming more elaborate, but there's ever less attention paid to the main figure: Man. It's partly due to this enormously high specialization, which is again, I'm very much afraid, a fault that belongs to the universities, which all encourage the kids to specialize and specialize with a vengeance. I am for specialization, but not at the expense of a wider knowledge, and that's what's happening. So the importance is the text of a funeral ceremony, the movements, the geography of it, the costuming of it, all the technical stuff. But how these people *feel* doesn't seem to enter into it."

Paul's constant emphasis was on the need for *communication* among scholars, world-wide. In this context he was interested in leading anthropology into fresh assessments of itself. Hence a large international conference, led by the then dean of American anthropologists, Alfred L. Kroeber, which resulted in a large encyclopedic inventory of knowledge called *Anthropology Today* (1953). And about the same time: *An Assessment of Anthropology Today* (1953). As a spinoff from this, in 1960 the Foundation established (Professor Sol Tax did most of the work) a journal called *Current Anthropology* which now has not only thousands of readers but also of associates in almost every country in the world. The principle of internationalism in scholarship has always remained central to the Foundation.

Another accomplishment was a brilliant interdisciplinary conference on *Man's Role in Changing the Face of the Earth*, held at Princeton in June 1952 (published in 1955). This was some time before the word "ecology" became fashionable, but the book is still a handbook for those interested in the relation of human beings to their natural environment.

In still another way he nudged anthropologists toward the use of new tools and instrumentations—or new interpretations of the old tools. The Foundation sponsored in 1961 a conference called "Ceramics and Man," the conception of which sprang from Paul and describes as well as anything else his approach to the study of man.

"This conference came about this way: I loathe one part of archeology and that is ceramics, because the artifact which, so to speak, survives is always clay; burned clay will survive x-thousand years. So this is what the archeologist jumps on. Many archeologists have a queer and utterly silly belief that it is no use to dig in tropical forests, because after 100 years or 200 years of burial in a wet, tropical forest, everything will disappear and only clay or stone will remain. Well, nothing disappears. The laws in chemistry for energy and for matter do remain, and no matter will disappear. But it is possible that, let's say, a leather bag buried possibly 200 years, would not be distinguishable any more for the archeologist as a leather bag. He will find something if he knows how to look for it, and if he knows a little bit of chemistry and a little bit of soil chemistry, then he can tell what the object was before. But most of them don't even know.

"So I came to hate ceramics because the archeologist decides to do typology on ceramics, and we have the most complicated hierarchy of ceramics—red on white, white on black, inside green and blue, and God knows what! The color and form in this is terrific—and you get very scientific-sounding classifications. In reality, they don't mean a thing and you can classify almost anything anywhere. But this became a cult in archeology, and there are heavy volumes written on it, libraries, and it doesn't lead anywhere. And in order to counteract this somewhat, I talked to Frederick Matson, who is an archeologist and was interested in ceramics, and said to him, 'Look, couldn't we once hold a conference on ceramics?' 'Oh, yes, yes.' I said, 'But not typology. Could we hold a conference on 'Ceramics and Man?' What is it that ceramics enabled man to do, because finally ceramics are responsible for our having cooked food, ceramics are responsible for our having animal husbandry, that we have domesticated plants (grain needed to be put somewhere). Let's start talking about this business. What is it that ceramics have done for man and what has man done with ceramics?' So this grew out of that. And it was a very good conference."

Paul believed that there was almost no problem without its possible solution. The trouble often was that the man who was asking the question didn't know where the answer was, and the man who had the answer had never heard the question. Paul's pressure toward communication, therefore, went beyond the customary scholarly interchanges. It involved the active reaching out of anthropology to chemistry, physics, astronomy, agriculture, medicine, biology—you name it—even to art, history, music, and philosophy. He always saw learning as a seamless garment. The effectiveness of such a program will always be limited by the available number of scholars equipped for and willing to engage in such broader and more difficult tasks. But the results extend enormously the effectiveness even of straight-line anthropology.

As early as 1947 Paul was sitting in his anthropological web luring in, because his inquiring mind was always making all sorts of connections, diverse talents for the solution of problems. In that year he brought paleo-anthropology and geophysics together, suggesting (successfully) that techniques used to locate

97

bodies of ore in the earth might also be used to locate ancient burials.

Perhaps the most brilliant certification of this interdisciplinary approach was in the discovery of Carbon-14 as a method of dating fossil remains. It came, as was so often the case with Paul, from a happy accident the results of which would never have been realized had there not been an alert mind poised to seize upon its implications.

The story has such historical interest that it is best to let him tell it as he recollected it, in his own vivid informal narrative:

"The same year, 1947, brought the birth of Carbon-14 dating. That happened right here at 14 E. 71st Street. We had imported from Java a Dutch paleo-anthropologist, Ralph von Koenigswald. He is famous as the one who found the *Java Man* and the *Gigantopithecus* and also the *Solo Man* and a number of others.

"It came about in this way. Franz Weidenreich, who was in the American Museum of Natural History, came to my office one day and told me that he had just got word from Java that Koenigswald was alive. He had been written off as dead after the Japanese invasion; he had disappeared. And then Weidenreich told me that Koenigswald had been caught by the Japanese, put into a concentration camp and was now free, *and* what was an important thing, his whole collection was intact. He succeeded in hiding all his skulls in different places in Java, and Weidenreich wanted aid to get him to the U.S. with his material. This was done.

"Because of the heat and humidity of the New York summer, Koenigswald moved out to the Cold Springs Harbor Lab, which had accommodations and was somewhat cooler than New York. He ate at their canteen, or lunchroom. At that time everybody at the laboratory was doing nuclear work, and people walked over to him and started to talk about nuclear physics and he didn't know what they were talking about. They always asked him, 'What are you doing here? How come you're here?' And he told them, 'I am a paleo-anthropologist.' But it seems that none of these physicists knew what a paleo-anthropologist was.

"Then one day *Life* came out with Koenigswald on the cover, with the *Solo* skull in his hand, and he brought it in very happily one afternoon and told me, 'Thank God this appeared, not because I want the publicity, but because from now on if any one of them asks what I am doing, I can give this to them.'

"And then he said a funny thing happened to him that day. Somebody sat at his table and asked him what he was doing, and he showed him this, and the guy pointed at the skull and said, 'How old is that?' So he said, 'Approximately half a million years.' This man then said, 'Too bad it is so old. If it were younger, I could have told you its exact age.'

"I said, 'Who was the guy?' 'I don't know.' 'What did he say? How could he tell it?' 'Oh,' he said, 'he talked something about radiation.'

"Now, just as the Good Lord gives luck sometimes, a day earlier I had been reading a book on geochronology and learned about the helium index, and how radium emanating at the end of it remains as helium. I got very much interested and said to Koenigswald, 'Who was the man with whom you talked?' He didn't know. So I called up my friend Demerech at Cold Springs Harbor on the phone and said, 'Could you do me a very big favor? It may sound funny, but I would like to know with whom Koenigswald had lunch. Could you send your secretary over to the lunchroom and try to find out whether one of the waiters might know?' So in half an hour's time the answer came back that Koenigswald had sat with Harold Urey. I did not know Dr. Urey personally at that time, but I knew of his work: Nobel Prize, discoverer of heavy water, and all that.

"So I called up the then President of the Foundation, Dick Hunt, and said this had happened, and I thought it was highly important, and I would like to follow this up and would like to commit the Foundation, if need be, for some money. Did I have his permission? So I got permission to commit the Foundation up to $25,000.

"Now I had to get together with Urey, whom I did not know. He was supposedly at Columbia at that time, so I called up Ralph Linton, who was also a professor at Columbia, and asked him if he knew Urey. He said, 'Yes, sure, we are on the same committee.' I said, 'Look, could you give me an introduction to him?' 'Oh, sure,' he said, 'I'll make an appointment and ring you back.' He

rang back thirty minutes later and said, 'Harold Urey left Columbia and is now at Chicago. As a matter of fact, he left this
afternoon on the Century.'

"So I called up Koenigswald and asked him if he was willing
to fly with me to Chicago the next morning, which he was, and
the next morning we arrived at Chicago before the Century got
there and waited at the railway station for Urey to get off. When
he got off, we walked over; Koenigswald introduced me and I
said to Urey that I was sorry to hold him up on the road, 'But
this sounds awfully important, though I don't know what's behind it. Could you tell me a little bit about what is involved?' So
he told me, 'Well, it is not I who does this, but I have an assistant,
a chemist, Dr. Willard Libby.' And Libby had found a carbon isotope, Carbon-14, in the sewage water of Baltimore. When
he found this in the sewage water, they started an investigation
with the Atomic Energy Commission and found out that no carbon isotope had been released; first, they thought that somebody
in a laboratory had poured it out into the sewage. But it did not
come from there. And then Libby made a long investigation into
where did it come from, and finally they found out that the
atmosphere contains Carbon-14, the carbon isotope. 'As the carbon isotope's half-life was known exactly,' he went on, 'I thought
that anything organic could be today analyzed for Carbon-14
emanation, and thereby used for determination of age.'

"By that time we were in a cab going towards Urey's lab, and
then I met Libby and told him that we were interested and that
the Foundation would be willing to underwrite some of the research. Now, Libby seemed reluctant. This was not something
which had been proved yet; he did not know if Carbon-14 emanation is constant over all parts of the earth, constant in time, and
all that. He felt that I was jumping on him too early. Nevertheless, I succeeded in unloading the $25,000 and we agreed that
he would continue working and when he knew that the emana-
tions are constant in all parts of the world, then we would start
working on it.

"Well, luckily, through the Antarctic Expedition of Byrd we
got samples from the Antarctic and also samples from many
other places, and after about three months, Libby told me, 'Yes,

it seems that way'—very carefully—'that maybe it is constant throughout.'

"So then he needed some more money to work out calculations and laboratory procedures and all that. I asked him if he would come over to New York and give us a paper on the Carbon-14 method. This is something that needs explanation. Every two weeks, on Fridays, there was always a Viking Fund Supper-Conference, which meant that we invited all the anthropologists on the Eastern Seaboard to come over here. At these affairs they got cocktails and dinner, and there was discussion until about 11 o'clock, and then they all went home. We paid their costs.

"So I asked him for one of these papers, and he consented to give it. And I asked him, 'When you write the paper, for God's sake go very easy on mathematics and physics, because the anthropologists are not up on it,' which he promised. He came over and gave a high talk on a rather low level—I think anybody could have understood it—but when the paper was finished, nobody rose for discussion. Nobody wanted to ask questions, nobody wanted to say anything. I even asked the anthropologists who were there, 'Don't you have something to say? Don't you want to know anything?' Nobody reacted. So it looked like a bad fizz-out.

"Then always the Lord is good somewhere. We had a non-anthropologist at the meeting, Richard Foster Flint from Yale University, who is a geologist. And Dick got up and looked at the anthropologists and said, 'Well, if you people are not interested in this, I am. I work in the Pleistocene and I can use the dating method. If *you* don't want anything to be dated, I am for it, and I would like to send some material. Where can I send it?'

"The moment Dick Flint said this, about ten people were already up: 'I would like to have my things dated; I have charcoal from Chile, and I want to date it.' And in ten seconds everyone wanted some things of their dated.

"Well, we agreed that I was unable to say which specimens should get the greatest priority, so a commission was elected from among the anthropologists, and it was decided that first museums should send in material with known dates. So things that were dated either by a historical method or other method should be sent first and let's see how it pans out.

"The specimens were sent over to the Foundation and I kept the data on the specimens, so that Libby never saw it, and we sent them out to him blind to date. Now, here is how a scientific method can be shown as good or bad. Among the materials provided, the Pennsylvania University Museum had sent a variety of materials. Among them was a piece of wood, which was duly numbered and sent out to Libby. Two weeks later Libby called me on the phone and said, 'I am sorry, but something must have gone wrong with my counter, because I am getting an entirely different date than on the rest of the material that you sent. And I suppose that this all belongs together but the dates are thousands of years apart. Could I get one more piece of that wood?' I said, 'I don't know. I'll find out.' And I called the Director of the Museum, Froelich Rainey, and asked Fro to send another piece of this because there's trouble with it. It developed that this piece of wood that they had thrown in was torn off from a packing case, and they had put it in as an afterthought—but deliberately.

"So I sent it to Libby and back came the determination that that piece of wood was 150 years old, plus or minus something. And, of course, this went around the profession almost overnight. Gossiping is strong in anthropology, and at the very first the anthropologists learned that they had tried to trick Libby and the thing didn't work; he gave the correct date. And at that minute, the method was holy. From then on, if anybody said the Carbon-14 date was such-and-such, it was accepted."*

*The following passage indicates the Foundation's interest in further dating methods, as shown in the *Twentieth Annual Report*, 1961, p. 29:
"In addition to the Carbon-14 dating method, research in the last decade has proceeded on the development of other supplementary means of determining the absolute or relative age of anthropological materials. The most well-known of these is the tree-ring dating technique. Grants have been awarded for the analysis of materials from the Rio Grande Valley, an area in which research has already provided a firm ground for the dating of specimens; and research was supported on the possibilities of dendrochronology in New Zealand. . . . Another method which has been developing in this period is the obsidian-hydration method, which takes advantage of the fact that due to the particular physical and chemical characteristics of obsidian, it appears as if the rate with which obsidian develops a rim of hydration

102

This man never influenced the course of anthropology? It could be said, to be sure, that if the world had waited, *somehow* the discoveries would have surfaced. This could be said, also, of the phonograph, or penicillin—or the wheel!

One other important program in physical anthropology was launched by Paul Fejos and given major support over the years for research, development, and distribution.

The only casts of skulls and bones of ancient man or of primates which had been available for study were made of plaster, and they were insufficiently accurate for any kind of refined study or research purposes. At the end of 1959, therefore, a grant was made to Mr. David Gilbert for the development of methods of making reproductions of anthropological specimens in plastic. These were not only less fragile than plaster casts; they were also much more accurate, so accurate that it took a trained eye to distinguish the reproduction from the original. As often happens in the development of new products, problems of manufacture and control arose in transferring the operation from laboratory to factory, and the Foundation spent what were for it large sums of money to perfect the process. At last, however, a

---

can be measured. Two grants supported this research, and progress has been made to the point of achieving reliable relative dates; absolute dating awaits further development but may be expected. The Foundation provided funds to aid the reestablishment of a laboratory for chemical dating at the University of California at Berkeley. A critical examination was concentrated on a few fossils of outstanding archeological significance, including Tepexpan from the Valley of Mexico. Materials and techniques were developed to analyze for water, nitrogen, carbonate carbon, organic carbon and fluoride, and in addition, because of the apparent persistence of nitrogen in fossil bones, exploratory investigations were done on the amino acids in bone protein. Support was given to the Research Laboratory for Archaeology, Oxford, by enabling the Laboratory to establish itself as a permanent department of the University and to embark on a program of developing and improving X-ray spectrometry dating technique. A geological dating technique which relies on established glacial sequences (which differ for each area under study) was aided in its development in a twofold program of basic research in the method itself, and simultaneous working out of the sequence of the glacial terraces at the Eden site, Wyoming. Two grants furthered the application of a technique for relative dating by geo-chemical analysis of soils."

Since 1961, the potassium-argon dating method—a "radio-isotopic clock" for identifying the geological age of rocks—has undergone refinements which bring its accuracy down to the upper limits of Carbon-14 dating: 40,000 to 50,000 years. Thus the two may be used to check each other concerning the age of certain materials. The potassium-argon method, of course, can identify and date the materials in rocks reaching back millions of years. It thus becomes of prime importance in determining the antiquity of the earliest Homonids.

wide range of these plastic casts, made from molds taken from rare museum specimens, was made available to educational institutions. Physical anthropolgy had a new and very effective teaching tool.

In 1945 The Viking Fund moved into its own building on East 71st Street, which has remained its central home ever since. By the time the Viking Fund had become The Wenner-Gren Foundation in 1951, its leadership in support of all kinds of anthropological endeavor was well established. Gradually, because the value of its capital funds had increased, there was more money to do more with.

So important had the international aspect of the Foundation become that it seemed essential to establish a European Center where summer conferences could be held with anthropologists in attendance from all over the world. Hunting for a possible location in Austria, Paul found in 1957 a place an hour-and-a-half's drive south of Vienna which seemed ideally practical for the Foundation's needs. It was also sufficiently other-worldly and romantic to appeal to what must have been, to the Fejosian ears, the distant beating of Magyar drums.

The castle Burg Wartenstein was owned by Prince Liechtenstein, who had used it as a hunting lodge until Hitler moved into Austria. The Russians had occupied it during the war and had broken out the windows and dismantled the one bathroom, but the basic structures of the old stone buildings and battlements had withstood all their depredations. The fabric was sound, the roof was good, and the price was modest. At the same time the Foundation acquired some contiguous farm buildings—the Meierei—which, when remodeled, gave additional rooms for guests.

The oldest part of the castle had been built in 1190; most of the buildings were constructed between the fifteenth and eighteenth centuries. It was planted high on the hills of the eastern Alps, not far from Semmering Pass. Its massive bulk, with its two towers, loomed up in the evening sun like a purple painting by Maxfield Parrish. It had over fifty rooms (give or take a few; no one ever really counted them). A good deal of modernization

A view of Burg Wartenstein, Austria. The European Conference Center for the Wenner-Gren Foundation since 1957.

was necessary if anthropologists were to have more comforts and facilities than the original Count Wartenstein. The Foundation commissioned Architect Richard Praun to renovate the castle and modernize its interiors. It was re-wired for electricity, central heating was put in, and sixteen bathrooms were installed. Simple but comfortable furnishings were acquired, and the main stairwell was decorated with the proper series of coats-of-arms. So the castle was in business, very idylically indeed in that beautiful countryside overlooking the valleys below and the mountains beyond. There was more than enough room to house the 18-20 people who proved to be the optimum number for each ten-day summer conference.

Paul took great delight in scrambling all over the place, overseeing its restoration and planning its furnishings and arrangements. He needed a conference table which would seat twenty people and be round in shape, so that everyone could see everyone else and there would be no questions of protocol in seating. It was made to order by carpenters in the nearby town of Gloggnitz. In Paul's mind any conference table in Europe needed to be covered with green felt; how to get a piece of seamless felt fifteen feet in diameter? It so happened that in Gloggnitz, of all places, was a felt factory which for scores of years had been turning out fezzes for the Middle East trade (a curious story in itself). So the green felt was made to specifications and properly installed.

There was a strong element of nostalgia in Paul's creating this conjunction of the baronial Middle Ages and modern academia. Austria, to be sure, was not the Austria of the Vienna waltzes before World War I when he had functioned as a member of the Palace Guard at the Hofburg in Vienna. But Wartenstein was enough to serve for him as another cocoon of the past. At almost every turn Paul's life was a series of paradoxes: in one sense he never looked behind him but shed one career in order to start a new one, eager only for the future. In another sense (and this became truer the older he got) his imagination lingered with the past, with his origins and the Europe he had known in his youth. When asked what he was politically he would say: "I am a monarchist." In truth his career, particularly because it had involved so much experience with the primitive natives he respected so highly, had made him a thoroughgoing believer in democracy—a belief rooted in what he had learned of the universal worthiness of the individual in whatever society. He seemed to become fully Americanized, and he was proud of his citizenship. But in his heart he always held the United States at a slight distance. He was more aware than most of the opportunities here; he was also aware of how much our expressed declarations of equality had failed to find true realization. He worried about the patched seams in the garment of the republic. It is true that he *was* apolitical, except as the dignity of man could become a matter of politics.

He had an instinct for making the fantastical serve utilitarian purposes. This was peculiarly true of Wartenstein. However deep its romantic pull may have been for him, it did prove the ideal place in which to bring anthropological minds together to spark new ideas and fresh perspectives. Part of the effectiveness lay in the comfortable and attractive (but imposed) isolation in which the conferees lived for ten days—with a one-day junket into the countryside to enable them to get away from each other. No other side-attractions, nothing except the congenial focus of scholars exploring for a time a common subject in the light of their multi-national and often muli-disciplinary approaches.

Much of the educational interchange went on in the halls and until late at night in the commons-rooms as well as at the conference table. To say nothing of the bar, for which conferees always have a territorial instinct.

Some of the new *aperçus* found their way into the publication of the conference papers. Many of them were unmeasurable in the sense that they would lie underground but might, in truth, induce a scholar to take a fresh look at his prejudices, or his convictions, to give them a gentler name. It could be very stimulating; it could also be unsettling, but the academic mind can frequently be shaken up with benefit to the profession. All this has been attested to by hundreds of scholars for whom conferences at Wartenstein have widened their whole intellectual horizon.

Beginning with the 1950s there was a great increase in anthropological interest in Africa. It was becoming increasingly clear to prehistorians that the cradle of man was there, not in Asia, as had been believed for so long. The earliest findings came under the general rubric of *Australopithecines*. A long and controversial search began for the earliest paleo-anthropological remains of hominids. In 1952 the Foundation established its Program on Early Man in Africa. It helped Professor Raymond Dart in South Africa. It modestly assisted Dr. L. S. B. Leakey in the earlier years of his indefatigable search for traces of early man—or his ancestors—at Olduvai Gorge in Tanzania and other sites. The work at Olduvai resulted in the discovery later on by his wife, Mary Leakey, of *Zinjanthropus boisei*. At the bottom of this deeply stratified gorge what seemed a possible precursor of early man had, as Paul put it, "been waiting quietly for one-and-three-quarters of a million years." The Foundation also supported field research in cultural anthropology in Africa by scholars from England, Australia, South Africa, and Portugal, as well as from the United States.

Paul always dated the beginnings of the Foundation's interest in early man in Africa by a paper read by Père Teilhard du Chardin at a Wenner-Gren conference in 1952, in which he declared his belief in the African origin of man—a far-out theory at that time. The Foundation had a very close relationship with Père Teilhard until his death. Paul revered him as one of the greatest intellects he had ever known, and one of the greatest men. The Foundation gave him early grant assistance, to say nothing of encouraging him through some of his very difficult years. He had an office in the building for some time.

Paul describes this as he recollected it:

"Père Teilhard was a thin, tall ascetic looking Jesuit, with a face I can describe only this way: a beautiful medieval saint. He had infinite elegance—hands which to watch was like looking at ballet. Every motion he made was superbly artistic and aesthetically beautiful. He spoke English with a French twang, and even that was utterly elegant. And of course his attractiveness did not end with his physical makeup. He had a fabulous soul, and he was not at all a bigot; he was a Frenchman, coming

108

from a very old family, a noble family in France; and he was a man, too.

"We got him in a very strange way. We gave a grant for Père Teilhard to go to Africa. It was a travel grant to go to South Africa to examine certain finds there, and when he came back he gave a paper at the Foundation. The paper was mostly about evolution, and a great number of things he said were a red flag to the Catholic Church. A Boston newspaper wrote about the heretical ideas of this French Jesuit in New York. As Père Teilhard later related the story to me, when he went back to France, he was called to task, first by the Provincial there. Then he was summoned to Rome, where again he was put through all the loops about his heretical teachings, and the Cardinal who was examining him got very impatient and said, 'But, my son, what are you searching for?' And Père Teilhard looked up and very solemnly said, 'Your Eminence, I am in search of a new God.' This shows a little bit who he was. I admit that today the Vatican couldn't strangle him, but 400 years before he would have been burned for this. And he didn't mean this disrespectfully; it was really his philosophy, that a new God is needed.

"He told me that when he returned to Paris, he was called to the Provincial, and was told, 'You are in bad grace. You must be disciplined and you must be able to see the truth. So as soon as this work for which you got money from the United States is finished, we will put you out in the Midi or somewhere out in the country, to a secular priest, a young and zealous one to keep you in line.' As a consequence of that, I got a letter from Père Teilhard asking for aid, which we gave. When he came here he told me the story.

"So we put Père Teilhard on a modest grant every year, which maintained his relationship to the Foundation. This was his only need because he lived in the Jesuit monastery on Park Avenue and did not need any money for himself. We kept renewing his grant as long as he lived.

"It was the greatest and cheapest investment we ever made. He was here with us for some three years, and then on Easter afternoon, 1955, he died suddenly of a heart attack.

"Later the Jesuits began to accept in part the great mind they had not exactly encouraged. Many of his writings appeared both in France and in the United States. Some of his works which had never been published came out, and the Jesuits remained a little uneasy."*

Paul and his wife Marianne were divorced in 1957. He then married in New York, late in 1958, Lita Binns, who had worked at the Foundation for some time and became, as his wife, his very able co-worker as well as his great psychological support in the later years. Mrs. Fejos (now Mrs. John Osmundsen) became Director of Research of the Foundation on Paul's death, and continues to direct its affairs with an alertness and efficiency of which Paul would have highly approved. There can be no greater tribute.

Paul's last few years were sad ones for himself and for all who knew him. The dynamo which had been his body began to give out; he was seized with a variety of afflictions and operations which limited his physical activity. He continued to manage foundation affairs, and even, in pain, to make the regular summer trips to Wartenstein. But he was burning out early, as life expectancies go. As a doctor he knew it and few people could feel more intensely the crippling effects of illness. His friends could only suffer with him silently.

He had collected all kinds of medals and honors along the way, beginning with both the first and second class silver and the bronze medals of valor from Austria-Hungary when he was

*Père Teilhard's reputation and influence did indeed mushroom spectacularly after his death. His first book to be published in the United States, in translation (1959), was *The Phenomenon of Man* (published four years earlier in France). It started what could almost be called a cult, and it was praised as the work of a remarkable man and a profound thinker even by those who disagreed with its premises and could not allow its conclusions. No one could fault his scientific eminence, though his evolutionary theories implicitly denied the current genetical theory of evolution. At most he believed that "the blind determinism of the genes played a subordinate part." He saw man both as a product and as a responsible participant. As one reviewer put it: "The thousand million years of evolution are seen here as one single act of creative power, like that revealed by Genesis. The creative act is inherent in the universe." But Teilhard was a poet as well as a scientist, and the more mystical passages of his later chapters confused some people as much as they inspired others. Metaphysics and science and poetry were fused in this work which, as Sir Julian Huxley said in his introduction to the American edition, "has forced theologians to view their ideas in the new perspective of evolution, and scientists to see the spiritual implications of their knowledge."

in the war in 1917. He had decorations from Turkey and Peru and Italy and Austria. He was awarded the 75th Anniversary University of Arizona Medal of Merit in 1960. Between 1950 and 1954 he was first the Vice-President and then the President of the New York Academy of Sciences. Being human, he enjoyed all these distinctions—quietly.

More and more his mind turned toward the old days in Europe; his nostalgia seemed to give him some support. He grew morose even about the state of anthropology, failing to realize fully that his own constructive efforts had helped a whole new generation of younger anthropologists think freshly about their discipline. His old friends, the great anthropologists with whom he had worked in the early days of the Foundation, had died. Ralph Linton, Alfred Kroeber, Alberto Blanc, Clyde Kluckhohn —giants all. The last three had died during the disastrous summer of 1960, which was also the summer of his mother's death in Hungary. This last disappearance of his ties with the past shook him greatly. He had always felt very close to his mother, though he had not been able to see her since before the Second World War. He could not be admitted to Hungary, and she would not leave, for she wanted to be buried next to her husband.*

At the end, Paul felt that the noble flair had gone out of life. He died on April 23, 1963.

As he had requested, his widow scattered his ashes from the towers of Wartenstein. The man so modern and yet so much a part of his past, had returned.

Early in this memoir I called Paul Fejos's life "unique"—a word so often used that it fails, I fear, to carry my full meaning. For everyone's life is unique in the sense that it is his alone. There was no one sector of Paul's career that did not have its parallels: there have been other fine directors of motion pictures, other adventurous explorers and ethnologists, other able presi-

*There was one ironic moment when Paul almost did return. In 1956 he received a phone call from the Minister of Education in Budapest, who had cleared an invitation for him to return to Hungary on a state visit. He was getting ready to go, when the revolution broke out the next week.

dents of philanthropical foundations. And Renaissance men did not entirely disappear into history with the Renaissance.

But Paul's multiple careers, as a constellation, the inner spark of creative imagination which informed each of them, and the overarching synthesis which this Hungarian-American brought to the world of learning as we know it—all this was his own and had its own inevitable inner logic, however illogical its presuppositions might have seemed at times.

Paul's tact, his instinctive perception of greatness, was almost infallible. He ran the Foundation as he directed a motion picture or conducted an exploring expedition: he was in complete control, with a feeling of total responsibility for all details, lest someone should allow the performance to be flawed. He did it with grace and dignity and great kindness and a sensitive awareness of the needs, physical and spiritual, of other people. Always he seemed to have on tap his great resources of knowledge in many fields, to bring them to bear upon some new construction of knowledge in a way which constitutes, in essence, the creative act.*

He was fond of Terence's statement: "I am a man, and nothing human is foreign to me." This could serve as his own complete epitaph. The record of his life was not just one of personal accomplishment; the clarity of his intuitions and the reach of his sympathies led other people toward greatness.

Anyone who knew him grew a little.

One epilogue, so amusing and dramatic and characteristic that only Paul Fejos could have staged it.

On a summer afternoon in August 1971, at the castle, Lita was expecting a visit from the Austrian artist Robert Fuchs, who had painted Paul's portrait earlier and was now doing sketches for a bronze plaque-portrait which would memorialize him at Wartenstein. The gate had been left open.

---

*This was true not only in the field of anthropology. Since for many years almost the entire holdings of the Foundation were in Electrolux stock, Paul was asked to sit on the Electrolux Board. It was a time when major administrative shifts were taking place in the corporation, and his fellow Board member, Mr. Charles J. R. Davis, remembers how acutely Paul sized up what was essentially a corporate business-and-personnel set of problems, and threw his weight on the side of probity and efficiency.

A car drove into the courtyard, but instead of Fuchs it disgorged two strangers, a man and a woman, who identified themselves in German as relatives, from Budapest, of Paul's first wife, Mara. They were, they said, on a pilgrimage "to see where Paul had worked." Lita was in the kitchen-building when they arrived; she took them across the courtyard into the lounge, where she served them coffee. Nobody had very much to say. Lita, though she was gracious, had in mind Paul's last command to her: "I forbid you to have anything to do with Hungarians—particularly any relatives of mine. They will suck the blood out of you!" He had had some bad experiences trying to send his relatives and friends clothes, medicines, and supplies to Hungary; they were less than appreciative. At the moment this all seemed a little amusing to Lita, if awkward.

As the couple finally started to leave it got darker, and within five minutes rain was coming down in a cloudburst, blindingly so. The visitors could barely make it, with umbrellas, across the courtyard to their car. They zoomed out of the courtyard and over the drawbridge. At that moment there was a flash of lightning, very close, accompanied by a terrific thunder-clap. The lightning had actually shot across the courtyard where the car had been, in through the kitchen window, and struck the rotisserie.

The intense rainstorm subsided quickly. Mrs. Haupt, the housekeeper, returned from attending a wedding in the nearby village of Gloggnitz, in the valley just below. Lita said: "Isn't it something about the lightning hitting the kitchen?" Mrs. Haupt said, in surprise, "Why, down in the valley it was all sunshine—not one cloud or drop of rain!"

Lita could only conclude the Herr President Fejos had been so angry with the visitors that he threw the bolt of lightning. He had always, when he lost his temper, been capable of throwing things! No movie could have been better directed; indeed the episode was reminiscent of an analagous scene in *Marie*.